A Note From Rick Renner

I am on a personal quest to see a "revival of the Bible" so people can establish their lives on a firm foundation that will stand strong and endure the test as end-time storm winds begin to intensify.

In order to experience a revival of the Bible in your personal life, it is important to take time each day to read, receive, and apply its truths to your life. James tells us that if we will continue in the perfect law of liberty — refusing to be forgetful hearers, but determined to be doers — we will be blessed in our ways. As you watch or listen to the programs in this series and work through this corresponding study guide, I trust you will search the Scriptures and allow the Holy Spirit to help you hear something new from God's Word that applies specifically to your life. I encourage you to be a doer of the Word He reveals to you. Whatever the cost, I assure you — it will be worth it.

> Thy words were found, and I did eat them;
> and thy word was unto me the joy and rejoicing of mine heart:
> for I am called by thy name, O Lord God of hosts.
> — Jeremiah 15:16

Your brother and friend in Jesus Christ,

Rick Renner

My Favorite Sparkling Gems
Ten Bible Teachings With Hidden Gems From the Greek

Copyright © 2023 by Rick Renner
1814 W. Tacoma St.
Broken Arrow, OK 74012-1406

Published by Rick Renner Ministries
www.renner.org

ISBN 13: 978-1-6675-0409-4

eBook ISBN 13: 978-1-6675-0410-0

How To Use This Study Guide

This ten-lesson study guide corresponds to *"My Favorite Sparkling Gems"* *With Rick Renner* (**Renner TV**). Each lesson in this study guide covers a topic that is addressed during the program series, with questions and references supplied to draw you deeper into your own private study of the Scriptures on this subject.

To derive the most benefit from this study guide, consider the following:

First, watch or listen to the program prior to working through the corresponding lesson in this guide. (Programs can also be viewed at **renner.org** by clicking on the Media/Archives links or on our Renner Ministries YouTube channel.)

Second, take the time to look up the scriptures included in each lesson. Prayerfully consider their application to your own life.

Third, use a journal or notebook to make note of your answers to each lesson's Study Questions and Practical Application challenges.

Fourth, invest specific time in prayer and in the Word of God to consult with the Holy Spirit. Write down the scriptures or insights He reveals to you.

Finally, take action! Whatever the Lord tells you to do according to His Word, do it.

For added insights on this subject, it is recommended that you obtain Rick Renner's books *Sparkling Gems From the Greek, Volumes 1* **and** *2*. You may also select from Rick's other available resources by placing your order at **renner.org** or by calling 1-800-742-5593

TOPIC

The Holy Spirit Knows How To Get You There Faster and Safer

Editor's Note: This lesson was taken from Rick Renner's *Sparkling Gems From the Greek, Volume 1*: January 10, July 3, September 1, and December 31. *Sparkling Gems From the Greek* is a daily devotional from the Greek language of the New Testament.

SCRIPTURES

1. **John 16:13** — Howbeit when he, the Spirit of truth, is come, he will guide you into all truth: for he shall not speak of himself; but whatsoever he shall hear, that shall he speak: and he will shew you things to come.

2. **Romans 8:14** — For as many as are led by the Spirit of God, they are the sons of God.

GREEK WORDS

1. "guide" — ὁδηγέω (*hodegeo*): a form of the Greek word ὁδός (*hodos*), which is the word for a road or a path; in this form, ὁδηγέω (*hodegeo*) depicts one who leads you down a road or path; a guide who leads you on an excursion

2. "led" — ἄγω (*ago*): I lead; in an agricultural sense, often depicted animals led by a rope tied around their necks and that followed wherever their owner led them; thus, to be led by a gentle tug or pull; also used in an athletic sense to describe an intense conflict; depicts two wrestlers struggling with each other

SYNOPSIS

The ten lessons in this study guide titled *My Favorite Sparkling Gems* will focus on the following topics:

• The Holy Spirit Knows How To Get You There Faster and Safer

- How To Experience Peace Even in Difficult Circumstances
- The Devil's Destination
- Telltale Signs That Bitterness Is Growing in Your Heart
- What Is a Cloud of Witnesses?
- On What Basis Will You Be Rewarded?
- It's Time for You To Start Using the Gifts and Talents God Gave You
- Perilous Times Shall Come
- Equipped To Sail Victorious Through Stormy Times
- Come Boldly to the Throne of Grace

The Holy Spirit is your Divine Guide. And not only is He your Guide, but He is also your Helper and Protector. The Holy Spirit already knows which paths you need to take, so when you listen to His guidance, you will be led to your destination safely and efficiently.

The emphasis of this lesson:

The Holy Spirit wants to take you through life with the benefit of His wisdom and guidance. He already knows the paths you should travel on and the stops you should take and how long you should take them. It is essential that you *trust* and *listen* to the Holy Spirit and pay close attention to those persistent tugs at your heart. As you listen and obey, He will make His voice known to you more and more. You will recognize His pull on your heart and trust that He will lead you in the right direction.

The Spirit of Truth

In John 16, Jesus was teaching His disciples about the ministry of the Holy Spirit when He said, "Howbeit when he, the Spirit of truth, is come…" (John 16:13). Jesus called the Holy Spirit the "Spirit of Truth" and referred to Him by this name — the Spirit of Truth — three times in John 14, 15, and 16. Jesus was driving into the hearts of His disciples — and you and me — that *the Holy Spirit can be trusted.*

The Holy Spirit will never mislead you — He is the Spirit of Truth. You can depend and rely on Him, and you can trust whatever He tells you to do. In other words, Jesus was saying to His disciples, "He is the Spirit of Truth, and this is what He will do." John 16:13 continues:

Howbeit when he, the Spirit of truth, is come, he will *guide* you into all truth: for he shall not speak of himself; but whatsoever he shall hear, that shall he speak: and he will shew you things to come.

The word "guide" here is the Greek word *hodegeo*, which comes from the Greek word *hodos*. This word *hodos* is most often depicted as *a road or path*. But when this particular form of *hodegeo* is used, it no longer depicts a road but *one who leads you down a road or path*. It describes *a guide who would lead you on an excursion*.

If you've ever been led by a professional guide, you know how important this person is to the success of the adventure. The guide knows all the sites, what's interesting and what's not interesting, and the right way to go to save you time and get you to the destination safer and faster. A knowledgeable and professional guide knows how to give you a really pleasurable experience. And if you'll trust your guide and follow his or her instructions, you will have a *marvelous* experience!

It is this word — translated as the word "guide" — that Jesus spoke in John 16:13. Jesus chose this word deliberately to convey the picture of the Holy Spirit as our professional Tour Guide who knows how to get us to our destination safely.

The Importance of a Good Guide

In the program, Rick shares the following story about the importance of having a good tour guide:

> I want to give you an example of the importance of a professional tour guide. I live in Moscow, Russia, and I have been through the Moscow Kremlin Armoury Museum countless times. And as a result, I could give you a pretty good tour of the Armoury Museum.
>
> There are other tour guides who will tell you things that aren't interesting and things that will bore you. They'll lead you this way and that way and your back will hurt by the time the tour is over because the floors are made of granite. Not only that, but there's only one restroom in the entire museum. So a good tour guide would tell you that you need to stop at this restroom because you wouldn't get another chance.

Well, if *I* was your tour guide, I would show you something *really* amazing. I would walk you through all the coronation dresses of the tsars and their wives. These pieces of clothing are just spectacular! The coronation dresses were spun of pure silver, and that's why their form has never changed over the years.

There's another gown that was worn by one of the priests of the church that has 168,000 pearls — *it's incredible!* Or how about the throne of Boris Godunov, or the throne of Ivan the Terrible, or the throne of the Romanovs, or the double-seated throne of Peter the Great and his brother?

And then I would walk you into the room where all the jewelry is held. They have jewelry that was once worn by horses. Yes, *horses!* When you come out of that room, I would tell you to hang to the right until you came upon the crowns that were used by the early Romanovs and Ivan the Great.

I would then take you to see a big, round room where you could walk through all of the carriages. In particular, the most splendid are the carriages of Empress Elizabeth the First, who was called "the party queen" of Russia. She *loved* parties. In fact, she made a rule that anyone who attended one of her extravagant balls in St. Petersburg could never wear the same dress again. And to make sure her guests never wore the same dress twice, her servants would stamp the back of the dresses with an ink blot.

And that's just the first floor of the museum!

We would then walk up the big steps that lead to the second floor of the Armoury where you can see all the ambassadorial gifts that were brought to the tsar. This sheds light on Proverbs 18:16, which says, "A man's gift makes room for him." No ambassador ever came to visit the tsar without bearing a gift because gifts literally opened doors for them. And let me tell you, that room in the museum is filled with the most splendid gifts.

I could go on and on and on, but there are a lot of things in the museum you wouldn't want to see. You can get *too much* information, and by the time you leave, you may also have a back or foot ache. But if I was your guide, and you really trusted me and listened to my instruction, I would give you an experience in that museum that you would never forget! By the time you left, you would be elated because of the experience you had due to having *a good guide.*

This entire concept of a professional tour guide is denoted within the word "guide," which again, is used in John 16:13. As previously mentioned, the word "guide" is translated from the Greek word *hodegeo,* which means that the Holy Spirit already knows every route you should take. He knows everything in front of you and every assault the devil has planned for you. The Holy Spirit knows how to get you to your destination faster and safer! My friend, if you will follow the leadership of the Holy Spirit, your walk with God will be *the most pleasurable adventure!*

Follow the Leader

The apostle Paul shed light on the leadership qualities of the Holy Spirit in the book of Romans. It says:

> **For as many are led by the Spirit of God, they are the sons of God.**
>
> **— Romans 8:14**

In this verse, we find that if you are a child of God, *you have the right to be led.* When you read this in the Greek language, the Greek structure is different. The *King James Version* says, "As many are led by the Spirit of God," but, in Greek, it actually says, "As many as by the Spirit of God are being led." It puts the Holy Spirit at the very first part of the verse, and we are *behind* Him — almost like tagalongs. The Holy Spirit wants to be out in front of your life, and you are to be a tagalong — *following His lead.*

When Rick was a boy, he and his siblings played the game Follow the Leader. His older sister, Ronda, always designated herself as the leader. Now, Ronda is very dear to Rick and they speak every day, but Ronda always said, "I'm the leader!" — especially when it was time to clean the house. She would say, "Rick, you're to do this, and Lori [Rick's other sister], you're to do that." Their job was to follow the leader, and they didn't dare argue with Ronda because she was older than them. They just "followed the leader" and did explicitly what they were told.

In this same way, the Holy Spirit wants to be the leader. He says, "Follow me, I'll tell you where to go and exactly what to do. You can trust me — I am the Spirit of Truth." You see, the Holy Spirit wants to be out front to safely guide you in *everything* you do.

The word "led" in Romans 8:14 is translated from the Greek word *ago* and has two meanings. First, *ago*, translated as "led," means *I lead*. In an athletic sense, it described *two wrestlers struggling with each other, one trying to throw the other to the mat.* The second meaning is used in an agricultural sense to describe *the moment when a farmer would place a rope around the neck of a cow, a mule, or a beast to lead them somewhere, and the beast would obediently follow.* Like the farmer leading the beast with a rope, you could say that the Holy Spirit has symbolically placed a rope around your neck, and He is gently tugging at it, *leading and guiding you.*

Many people might like to see a bright flash of lightning or have a divine dream during the night, but the Holy Spirit doesn't usually lead that way. Most often, He simply tugs on your heart — you just have to be sensitive to listen to it. In fact, the tugging of the Holy Spirit is sometimes *so gentle* you might miss or dismiss it as just a passing thought. But the Holy Spirit is tugging; He's trying to pull us in the right direction. And as the sons and daughters of God, we must pay attention to that tugging in our hearts.

A Wrestling Match To Remember

The second meaning of the word "led," the Greek word *ago*, was used as an athletic term to describe *a wrestling match*. Sometimes the pull of the Holy Spirit may throw us into a wrestling match. We can know in our heart that the Holy Spirit is telling us to do something, but our mind may be telling us, *This can't be right! Certainly, the Holy Spirit isn't telling me this!* A wrestling match takes place between our spirit and our mind. In those moments, we have to choose to submit our minds to the leadership of the Holy Spirit.

In the program, Rick shares a story about a time when his flesh wrestled with the pull of the Holy Spirit on his heart:

> Many years ago, Denise and I were ministering at a meeting in the city of Chicago. We had been to every meeting, our friends were preaching, and we were having such a good time!
>
> One day after the morning meeting, Denise and I went back to our hotel to take a nap. And as I lay there trying to sleep, I felt

inwardly disturbed, and I recognized the Holy Spirit was trying to tell me something. I felt that tug on my heart, and I felt the Holy Spirit leading me, pulling on my heart that I was to skip the evening meeting, stay in the hotel, and not leave the room.

This instruction seemed so weird to me — *Why would the Holy Spirit tell me to stay in the room?* And I actually said to Denise, "I don't know why, but for some reason I feel like I'm supposed to stay in the room tonight while you go to the evening service."

I struggled with it. It was a real wrestling match between my mind and my spirit. Finally, I said to Denise, "I'm just going to dismiss this. There's no reason I can think of why God would want me to stay in the hotel room tonight." I started getting ready for the meeting when suddenly there was a knock on our door.

I thought it was our driver who had come to pick us up at the hotel. So I yelled in reply, "Hey! I'll be ready in just a few moments! We're running a little late, but we'll be out soon!" I dressed quickly and went to open the door, but there was no one there. I said to Denise, "I think the driver is downstairs waiting for us. I'm going to go downstairs and tell him you'll be down in just a minute."

But when I got downstairs, our driver wasn't there. In fact, our driver was running late. Finally, the driver pulled up and once Denise came down, we both got into the car. We headed across the city of Chicago to the meeting, and the whole way I was inwardly disturbed because I kept thinking, *You've got to stay in the room.* Sometimes it's a thought; sometimes it's a tug on your heart.

I kept having the thought, *Why did you leave the room? I explicitly told you to stay in the room!*

But my mind was saying, *Why? Why would the Holy Spirit tell me to stay in the room while the glory of God is going to be poured out in this meeting tonight? That's where I want to be!*

Still, I kept feeling this tug to stay in the hotel room. So I said to Denise, "I don't know what I should do. Should I go? Should I turn around?" We drove for a few more miles when the driver got involved in our conversation. He said, "Mr. Renner, if you wish, I will turn the car around and take you back to the hotel." I was embarrassed because I was wavering back and forth. I finally said, "No, just go to the meeting."

So we went to the meeting and walked into the green room where all the speakers were and greeted everyone. And when they turned to walk into the auditorium for the meeting, I looked at Denise and said, "I'll see you later. I don't know why, but I just have to go back to the room. *I have to be in that room tonight.*"

I got in the car and the driver started taking me back across Chicago to my hotel room. We were almost at the hotel when I remembered I had missed dinner! So I asked the driver to stop at a fast-food place and let me run in and get a hamburger. He stopped, and I went in to get my hamburger. And then I saw that there was a convenience store across the parking lot, so I walked over and went in to get toothpaste. Eventually, I got back into the car and asked the driver to take me back to the hotel.

When I arrived, the attendant at the registration desk said, "Oh, you're back so early! Is the meeting finished? Why did you come back early?" I didn't even know how to respond. What was I supposed to say? *Oh, I just feel like I'm supposed to be in the room tonight.* There *really* was a struggle going on between my mind and my spirit.

I walked onto the elevator, punched the button to my floor, went up to my room, walked down the hall, opened the door, and stepped inside. *Lo and behold* — our room looked like a tornado had been through it! Our suitcases were open, and our clothes were laying all over the room. My computer bag had been gone through and my computer was gone. Our passports were gone. Denise's jewelry bag was open and completely empty. All of her jewelry was gone. *Everything* was gone. I realized we had been robbed.

As I was standing there in the middle of our ransacked room, I heard the Holy Spirit say, "Now you know why I told you to stay in the room." If I had stayed in my hotel room that night, the robbery would not have happened. And do you remember that little knock at the door? That was the thief who had come to see if we were still there or if the coast was clear to invade our room, ransack it, and rob us.

If I had listened to the tugging on my heart and stayed in the room, no one would have broken into the room. And later that night when Denise would have come back from the meeting, I probably would have said, "You know, I stayed in the room. I don't know why, but I'm glad I did."

That night, Rick realized there had been many instances when the Holy Spirit had led him to do things and he had obeyed, even though he never really knew why. But because he obeyed, he avoided something negative. In Romans 8:14, we are reminded that we are to be *led* by the Holy Spirit; He will tug on our hearts. Just like the Greek word *ago* has a dual meaning — to lead an animal by a rope and a wrestling match — the Holy Spirit wants to gently guide us down the right path, and He wants to help us win the battles between our mind and our spirit.

In order to truly be led by the Holy Spirit, we must submit to our spirit and deny our mind, so He can guide and instruct our every step. And if we listen to Him, the Holy Spirit will safely get us where we need to go and avoid the traps that the enemy has set for us.

STUDY QUESTIONS

Study to shew thyself approved unto God, a workman that needeth not to be ashamed, rightly dividing the word of truth.
— 2 Timothy 2:15

1. What is the significance of Jesus calling the Holy Spirit "the Spirit of Truth" three separate times in the gospel of John?

2. Can you think of a time when you knew the Holy Spirit was leading you to do something? Did you submit yourself to the leading of the Holy Spirit and obey His direction? Or did you shrug it off and submit to your flesh instead?

3. Take a moment to write down the meanings of the Greek word for "led." How does its dual meaning correlate with the ways in which the Holy Spirit tugs at your heart?

PRACTICAL APPLICATION

> But be ye doers of the word, and not hearers only,
> deceiving your own selves.
> —James 1:22

1. What are some ways you can train yourself to become more sensitive to the pull of the Holy Spirit? Write down these ideas and make a plan to incorporate them into your routine.

2. Have you ever received direction from the Holy Spirit that your flesh questioned and wrestled with, but as soon as you submitted yourself to His guidance, you found out exactly why the Holy Spirit led you in that direction? What did you learn from this?

3. Think about how much help is available to you through the Spirit of God within you. Make it a point today to thank Him for being your Helper and Friend!

LESSON 2

TOPIC

How To Experience Peace Even in Difficult Circumstances

Editor's Note: This lesson was taken from Rick Renner's *Sparkling Gems From the Greek, Volume 1:* April 8 - April 12. *Sparkling Gems From the Greek* is a daily devotional from the Greek language of the New Testament.

SCRIPTURES

1. **Psalm 119:18** — Open thou mine eyes, that I may behold wondrous things out of thy law.

2. **Luke 22:41** — And he was withdrawn from them about a stone's cast, and kneeled down, and prayed…

3. **Luke 22:42** — Saying, Father, if thou be willing, remove this cup from me: nevertheless not my will, but thine, be done.

4. **Luke 22:43,44** — And there appeared an angel unto him from heaven, strengthening him. And being in an agony he prayed more

earnestly: and his sweat was as it were great drops of blood falling down to the ground.

5. **John 18:2,3** — And Judas also, which betrayed him, knew the place: for Jesus oftentimes resorted thither with his disciples. Judas then, having received a band of men and officers from the chief priests and Pharisees, cometh thither with lanterns and torches and weapons.

6. **John 18:4,5** — Jesus therefore, knowing all things that should come upon him, went forth, and said unto them, Whom seek ye? They answered him, Jesus of Nazareth. Jesus saith unto them, I am he. And Judas also, which betrayed him, stood with them.

7. **John 18:6** — As soon then as he had said unto them, I am he, they went backward, and fell to the ground.

8. **John 18:10** — Then Simon Peter having a sword drew it, and smote the high priest's servant, and cut off his right ear. The servant's name was Malchus.

9. **Mark 14:50** — And they all forsook him, and fled.

10. **Mark 14:51,52** — And there followed him a certain young man, having a linen cloth cast about his naked body; and the young man laid hold on him: And he left the linen cloth, and fled from them naked.

11. **Mark 14:53** — And they led Jesus away to the high priest: and with him were assembled all the chief priests and the elders and the scribes.

GREEK WORDS

1. "agony" — **ἀγωνία** (*agonidzo*): a struggle; a fight; great exertion or effort

2. "earnestly" — **ἐκτενής** (*ektenes*): to be extended; to be stretched out

3. "band" — **σπεῖρα** (*speira*): a Roman military cohort

4. "he" — **Ἐγώ εἰμι** (*Ego eimi*): I AM!

5. "cut off" — **ἀποκόπτω** (*apokopto*): a compound of the words *apo*, meaning away, and *kopto*, meaning to cut downward; combined, *apokopto* describes a downward swing that severs or cuts off something

6. "led" — **ἄγω** (*ago*): to lead: often depicted an animal led by a rope tied around the neck, following wherever the owner led

In this lesson, we will find out just who the naked boy in the Garden of Gethsemane was and his significance to the events that unfolded when soldiers came to arrest Jesus as He was praying in the Garden of Gethsemane. Many important events took place in the Garden of Gethsemane during that momentous time. Jesus experienced the height of mental and emotional agony, yet He remained surrendered to the plan of God. He experienced ultimate betrayal and desertion, yet Jesus made himself available to the Father and demonstrated incredible manifestations of power. Each event — from Jesus' prayer to his surrender and arrest — played a significant part in the overall plan of God.

The emphasis of this lesson:

When Jesus was ambushed by soldiers and officers, led to the Garden of Gethsemane by Judas, He could have fought back. Jesus could have called upon an *army* of angels to save Him — but He didn't. Even in this high-stakes situation, Jesus looked to His Father and surrendered Himself to the plan of God. Just like Jesus, when you are faced with a difficult situation, wholly surrender yourself to the plan of the Lord and experience His perfect peace and power.

Jesus' Battle With the Agony of His Flesh and Betrayal

The power of God is irresistible — especially to the enemy. In this lesson, we'll look at an example of this divine power from the New Testament, beginning with the scene of Jesus praying in the Garden of Gethsemane in Luke 22:41. It reads:

> **And he was withdrawn from them about a stone's cast, and kneeled down, and prayed…**

Jesus had just finished an important conversation with His disciples about the events that were about to take place. After that conversation, He left them, walking about "a stone's cast" distance away, which indicates He didn't walk very far.

The *King James Version* religiously translated the next phrase, "…Jesus kneeled down, and prayed…." But those words "kneeled down" means He *collapsed*. Jesus was under extreme pressure as He was entering the greatest spiritual warfare He had ever encountered in His life. So Jesus prayed,

"Father, if thou be willing, remove this cup from me: nevertheless not my will, but thine, be done" (Luke 22:42).

Here we find there was a conflict in Jesus because His spirit was being led to the Cross, but His flesh was saying *no, no, no!* And as we saw in the last lesson, when we're led by the Spirit, there are times when our flesh will put up a fight. Jesus was in the fight of His life, realizing the Holy Spirit was leading Him to the Cross. And Jesus cried out and said, *"Father, if there's any other way."*

If you study the gospels of Matthew, Mark, and Luke comparatively, you'll find that Jesus prayed this prayer *three times*. Finally, He said, "Not my will, but Yours be done." Jesus *completely affirmed* His surrender to the plan of God.

The Bible goes on in Luke 22:43 and 44 to say:

> **And there appeared an angel unto him from heaven, strengthening him. And being in an agony he prayed more earnestly....**

The word translated "agony" is the Greek word *agonidzo*, and it's where we get the word "agony." This was an agonizing moment for Jesus; in fact, it was so agonizing that the *King James* translation says "He prayed more earnestly" (*see* Luke 22:44). This word "earnestly" in Greek is the word *ektenes*, and it describes *a person who is under such agony that he's writhing and rolling around, holding himself as if he's in excruciating pain.* This means Jesus was not just religiously on His knees praying with His hands put together — Jesus was *literally* sprawled out on the ground as He was writhing in agony, wrestling with what was about to unfold before Him.

In fact, His battle was *so intense* that an angel appeared to strengthen Him. Verse 44 continues:

> **... and his sweat was as it were great drops of blood falling down to the ground.**

This phrase "great drops of blood" is very important because it tells us just how intense Jesus' spiritual battle was.

This "sweating drops of blood" is actually a medical condition that still exists today, but it's very rare. This phenomenon occurs when a person is under such pressure mentally and emotionally that his body responds as if it's under real *physical* pressure. In fact, the perceived pressure is so great that the top and second layers of skin begin to separate, forming a vacuum which then fills with blood. That vacuum becomes *so full* that blood begins to ooze out through the pores of the skin.

A Roman Cohort Is Slain in the Spirit

Jesus was under such intense pressure spiritually that His body reacted as if it were under real physical pressure, causing His pores to ooze with blood. In John 18, we find what happens next in these critical moments in the Garden.

> **And Judas also, which betrayed him, knew the place: for Jesus ofttimes resorted thither with his disciples. Judas then, having received a band of men….**
>
> — **John 18:2,3**

The word "band" is the Greek word *speira*. This word isn't describing a couple of soldiers; the word *speira* describes a *Roman cohort*. A cohort was anywhere between *300* and *600* soldiers! Think about it, — Jesus' power was so legendary and immense, they knew it would take 300 to 600 soldiers to arrest Him! *They all knew about the power of Jesus!*

So Judas came with 300 to 600 men, including soldiers as well as officers from the chief priests and Pharisees. They came with lanterns, torches, and weapons. They were ready to put up a fight because Judas had warned them all in advance — *you simply can't comprehend the degree of power that operated through Jesus during His time among this group of people!*

These soldiers and court officials came with weapons in case Jesus chose to put up a fight. And they came with lanterns and torches in case Jesus chose to hide in the rocks, the caves, or the graves in the Garden of Gethsemane. But, of course, Jesus didn't do any of that.

The Bible tells us in John 18:4 and 5 what Jesus did instead. It reads:

> **Jesus therefore, knowing all things that should come upon him, went forth, and said unto them, Whom seek ye? They answered him, Jesus of Nazareth. Jesus saith unto them, I am *he*….**

That's what the *King James Version* says, and if you look at this verse in that translation, you'll notice the word "he" is italicized, which means it was added by the translators; it does not appear in the original Greek. What's amazing about this is, in the Greek language, "I am" is *Ego eimi*, which simply means *I AM!* These were exactly the same words God used at Mount Horeb in Exodus 3 when He explained to Moses who He was.

It was the equivalent of Jesus saying, "You're seeking Jesus of Nazareth? Let me tell you who I really am. *I AM!*" Jesus was declaring that He was God in the flesh. They came into the Garden saying, "We're seeking Jesus of Nazareth." And Jesus said in reply, "*I am. [Ego eimi.] I am the Great I AM!*"

Notice what the Bible says in John 18:5:

And Judas also, which betrayed him, stood with them.

Judas was standing with those who came to arrest Jesus. Verse 6 goes on to say:

As soon then as he had said unto them, I am *he*, they went backward, and fell to the ground.

This means that when Jesus spoke those words, there was a blast of power *so great*, they could not resist the power of Jesus Christ. Here we have a picture of 300 to 600 men — some of them soldiers and some of them officers from the chief priests — and among them was Judas Iscariot. All of them were blasted backward by the power that was released when Jesus said, "I AM!," and they fell to the ground or were what we often refer to as "slain in the Spirit" — powerless to resist the mighty power of God and could therefore not remaining standing under the "weightiness" of His glory.

Peter's Impulse and a Miracle for the Enemy

Right in the middle of this moment, Peter did something out of impulse. In John 18:10, the Bible tells us:

Then Simon Peter having a sword drew it, and smote the high priest's servant, and cut off his right ear. The servant's name was Malchus.

Simon Peter probably didn't like Malchus because he had likely heard Malchus on previous occasions say bad things about Jesus. Malchus was the public spokesperson of the high priests, and as such, he had most likely said many bad things about Jesus. So when Peter saw Malchus lying on the ground, dazed by the power of God, Peter thought, *I'm going to get him.* Peter drew a sword and cut off Malchus' ear.

The words "cut off" in Greek mean that he slashed it hard. But ask yourself, *If Peter was really trying to injure someone, would he deliberately aim for just the ear?* Probably not. He probably would have aimed for the head. And we know from the Bible that Peter was a fisherman, not a soldier. He likely wasn't very skillful with a sword. He swung for Malchus' head, but cut off his ear instead.

Remember, Malchus was the public spokesperson of the chief priests, so for Peter to cut off his ear was a *serious* offense. In fact, it was such a serious offense that Peter could have been executed or sent to prison for the rest of his life! When we read the other gospels, we see that Jesus said, "Give Me a minute" and then laid his hands on Malchus' head and healed him. What the Bible does not tell us is whether Jesus picked up the severed ear and put it back on, or if He just placed His hand on Malchus' head and grew him a brand-new ear. But here we find Jesus, in the moment of His arrest, demonstrating the amazing power of Christ by blowing every soldier, high-priest official, and Judas Iscariot onto their backs — and then performing a miracle on behalf of a prescribed enemy!

Jesus intervened when Peter was moved by his flesh to cut off the ear of Malchus. The point is, *amazing power* was in manifestation at the moment of Jesus' arrest. And that's not even the end of the story!

The 'Naked Boy' in the Garden — an Accidental Resurrection

There's an account in the gospel of Mark that scholars have struggled with because it's very strange. It begins in Mark 14:50, which says, "And they all forsook him, and fled."

So now Jesus has been arrested and His disciples have all forsaken Him and fled. Malchus has blood all over his head where Peter had taken off his ear. The soldiers are still dazed by the power of God. All these things have just taken place when, suddenly, something astounding happens:

> **And there followed him a certain young man, having a linen cloth cast about his naked body; and the young men laid hold on him: And he left the linen cloth, and fled from them naked.**
> **— Mark 14:51,52**

In providing commentary on these verses, it's easy to see how scholars can sometimes come to bizarre conclusions. Many couldn't figure out who the naked young man was in the Garden of Gethsemane. Some tried to say it was John, but why would John be running around naked in the Garden of Gethsemane?

You have to really dig into the text to find out who this naked young man was. The key to this mystery is in the words "linen cloth." These words were very specific and only used in one way — and, therefore, can only be translated in one way. The words "linen cloth" describe *a burial shroud*. A burial shroud was used for those who were very rich. These shrouds were made of linen imported from Egypt, and the wealthy were buried in this type of shroud.

The Garden of Gethsemane was filled with ancient tombs, as well as modern tombs that were contemporary at the time of this event. We find that when Jesus said, "I AM," and that power blew all those men backward onto the ground, that same power also touched a dead boy who had just been buried in his tomb and covered in a linen cloth, or burial shroud.

At the very moment the soldiers were wrapping a rope around Jesus' neck to take Him to be tried, this young man was raised from the dead and came crawling out of his tomb holding his burial shroud. All this young man knew was that he'd been raised from the dead. He didn't know what was going on. He was just holding the shroud that he had been buried with. And the Bible says when the soldiers saw that he had been raised from the dead, they laid hold of him (*see* Mark 14:51). In other words, they were probably thinking, *Get that kid! We don't need another rumor of a resurrection!*

Again, Mark 14:52 states, "And he left the linen cloth, and fled from them naked." The young man got away from them. He fled from them naked, and the same soldiers who thought they had the power and authority to arrest Jesus were standing there, holding the burial shroud of a boy who had just been raised from the dead. Rick Renner likes to call this a *periphery* or an *accidental resurrection* because it wasn't Jesus' intention, but that's how much power Jesus manifested.

When the power in Jesus was in manifestation, *all kinds* of things took place! The reason all this is so important is because of Mark 14:53, which reads:

> **And they led Jesus away to the high priest: and with him were assembled all the chief priests and the elders and the scribes.**

The word "led" is the Greek word *ago*, which means *to lead*; and it often depicts *an animal led by a rope tied around the neck, following wherever the owner leads*. We're told in Isaiah 53 that Jesus was led like a lamb to the slaughter. But they didn't *take* Jesus — Jesus availed Himself to the plan of God and surrendered to the Father. He had *so much power* that with a mere word from His mouth, He knocked down all who were present at the Garden of Gethsemane flat on their backs. They were dazed under the power of God. Jesus then put His hand on the side of Malchus' face and either re-grew his ear or created for him a brand-new ear. Jesus manifested so much power in that garden that a dead boy who had just been buried came crawling out of his grave, carrying his burial shroud — completely raised from the dead by a periphery, or accidental, resurrection. *That is amazing!*

Jesus Surrenders

Not only that, but Jesus even said that if He had wished, He could have called on 12 legions of angels at that very moment, which is *144,000* angels! Those soldiers didn't have the authority or the power to take Jesus — they could only lead Him away because *Jesus surrendered.*

Jesus was being led to the Cross, but He won the battle of His will in the Garden of Gethsemane when He said to the Father, "Not my will, but thy will be done." And because of that, when the soldiers showed up, even though Jesus had the power to resist it all, He *allowed* them to wrap that rope around His neck. Jesus knew that, in reality, He was being led not by soldiers, but by the Spirit of God.

Jesus was led to stand trial before Pilate and was scourged, flogged, and eventually crucified. Jesus knew He had been born to be the Lamb of God and to take away the sins of the world. And at the moment when they came to take Him, even they couldn't resist the mighty power of Jesus.

That same power of Jesus Christ is available to you today, which means if anything is giving you a problem, just like Jesus said, "I AM," if you will speak the Word of God, *volumes* of power will be released to undo the attack of the enemy.

STUDY QUESTIONS

Study to shew thyself approved unto God, a workman that needeth not to be ashamed, rightly dividing the word of truth.
— 2 Timothy 2:15

1. Jesus was betrayed, ambushed, and arrested in a short period of time and was under such a great deal of stress that blood oozed from His pores. And still, He maintained a state of peace during all of this. How does Jesus' composure during this high-stress speak to you about how to stay in peace? What can you incorporate into your life from this story?

2. Did you know about the naked boy in the Garden of Gethsemane? What did you learn from his story?

PRACTICAL APPLICATION

But be doers of the word, and not hearers only, deceiving your own selves.
—James 1:22

1. Think of how Jesus answered the soldiers when they came asking about Him. How does the confidence of Jesus' reply, "I am," encourage you? Think of some "I am" phrases (concerning who you are in or because of Christ) that you can confess when in difficult situations. Write out two or three of them to meditate on and memorize.

2. Think about how Jesus redeemed Peter's act of impulse by healing Malchus' ear. Has the Lord ever done this for you in your life? Reflect on these instances.

3. There was an abundance of power available to Jesus in the Garden of Gethsemane. With this in mind, how does this influence your expectations for God's power to work in your own life?

TOPIC

The Devil's Destination

Editor's Note: This lesson was taken from Rick Renner's *Sparkling Gems From the Greek, Volume 1*: August 26. *Sparkling Gems From the Greek* is a daily devotional from the Greek language of the New Testament.

SCRIPTURES

1. **Ephesians 6:11** — Put on the whole armour of God, that ye may able to stand against the wiles of the devil.

2. **2 Corinthians 2:11** — Lest Satan should get an advantage of us: for we are not ignorant of his devices.

3. **2 Corinthians 10:4,5** — (For the weapons of our warfare are not carnal, but mighty through God to the pulling down of strong holds;) Casting down imaginations, and every high thing that exalteth itself against the knowledge of God, and bringing into captivity every thought to the obedience of Christ.

4. **Acts 10:38** — How God anointed Jesus of Nazareth with the Holy Ghost and with power: who went about doing good, and healing all that were oppressed of the devil; for God was with him.

GREEK WORDS

1. "devil" — **διάβολος** (*diabolos*): a compound of the preposition (*dia*), meaning through, and (*ballos*), meaning to strike or throw something over and over again; combined, *diabolos* describes the way in which the devil operates; one who repetitiously strikes until successfully penetrating an object to ruin it, affect it, or take it captive; to slander, accuse, or defame; to penetrate by continuous assault

2. "wiles" — **μεθοδεία** (*methodeia*): a compound of the preposition (*meta*), meaning with, and (*hodos*), which is the word for a road, path, or avenue; combined, *methodeia* describes one who operates with or travels on a road

3. "devices" — **νόηματα** (*noemata*): a form of the word (*nous*), the Greek word for the mind or the intellect; denotes the devil's plot to fill the human mind with confusion

4. "stronghold" — **ὀχύρωμα** (*ochuroma*): castle or fortress; the Greek word for prison; pictures a dreadful prison constructed deep inside a fortress that was intended to prevent a hostage or prisoner from escaping

5. "oppressed" — **καταδυναστεύω** (*katadunasteuo*): a compound of (*kata*) and (*dunamis*); the word (*kata*) carries the idea of domination; the word (*dunamis*) depicts a dominating tyrant; when compounded, it pictures the oppressive power of a tyrant or a wicked king lording himself over his subjects

SYNOPSIS

The devil is a tyrant whose sole purpose is to attack your mind and enslave you. He knows if he can control what you think, then he can control what you believe about yourself and your gifts, talents, and abilities. But you can learn how to stop the devil in his tracks and prevent him from reaching his destination: your mind.

The emphasis of this lesson:

The devil comes with lies, insinuations, and allegations to attack your mind. If you believe his lies, the devil can gain access to your mind and enslave and confuse you. But if you say 'no' to the devil and his advances and say 'yes' to the Lord and His Word, you can break free from the devil's shackles and be open to hearing what the Word of God has to say about your future!

Know How the Devil Operates

The devil's destination is your mind. He knows if he can enslave your mind and emotions, then he can begin to take you down. In Ephesians 6:11, Paul informed us how the devil operates. He said, "Put on the whole armour of God, that ye may be able to stand against the *wiles* of the *devil*."

The name "devil" is translated from the Greek word *diabolos*. It is a compound of the preposition *dia*, which means *through*, and carries the idea *of complete and total penetration*. The second part of the word *diabolos* is *bolos*, which is derived from the Greek word *bolo*, and pictures *throwing*

or striking something over and over again. When these words are compounded to form *diabolos* — translated as "devil" — it describes how the
enemy operates. The devil comes at his victims with his lies, allegations,
and insinuations and begins to strike their minds, again and again. It
pictures the devil striking his victim with lie after lie after lie, until finally,
he penetrates the mind.

The devil's intention is to penetrate the mind completely and thoroughly.
That's why the apostle Paul warns us to put on the whole armor of God
so we can "stand against the *wiles* of the devil" (Ephesians 6:11). The
word "wiles" is a translation from the Greek word *methodeia*, which is a
compound of the preposition *meta*, which means *with*, and the word *hodos*,
which is the word for *a road or a path*. Combined, *methodeia* describes one
who operates with or travels on a road. The devil is like a traveler on a road
that has one destination — your mind.

That's what this word "wiles" (*methodeia*) means. It tells us that the devil
will continue striking the mind, over and over with lies and accusations,
trying to wear it down, until finally, he gains entrance. And once he has
found that place of penetration, he methodically paves a road into the
mind which gives him free access to that person's mind and emotions.

The devil understands that the mind is the control center of your life.
What you think will determine what you believe and what you believe
about yourself. And if the devil can take you down in your mind, then he
can affect your self-image, the way you project yourself to others, and even
how others perceive you! He knows if he can just get into your head and
pave a road of access into it, then he will have the ability to scramble your
thoughts and emotions and attempt to take you down.

The Devil Wants To Build a Stronghold in Your Mind

In Second Corinthians 2:11, the apostle Paul wrote, "Lest Satan should
get an advantage of us: for we are not ignorant of his *devices.*" The word
"devices" in the Greek language is the word *noemata*, a derivative of the
word *nous.* The word *nous* is the Greek word for *the mind,* and it encom-
passes the mind, will, and emotions — the intellect. But when the word
nous becomes *noemata*, it's no longer just describing the mind, but *a mind
that's confused.*

And that is what the devil does to people. First, he strikes the mind. Then
he paves a road into the mind. And when he has access into the mind, he

goes to work to mentally confuse a person so they no longer understand what is reality and what is a delusion — they can no longer discern what's right from what's wrong.

Paul continued his illumination of the devil's intent in Second Corinthians 10:4. Paul said, "(For the weapons of our warfare are not carnal, but mighty through God to the pulling down of *strong holds*.)"

The devil wants to build strongholds in the mind. The word "stronghold" is the Greek word *ochuroma*, which describes *a castle* or *a fortress*, but interestingly, *ochuroma* is also the Greek word for *a prison*. Well, a castle serves one purpose, and a prison serves another purpose. A castle has big, thick walls that keep people on the outside, whereas a prison has bars that keep people on the inside and behind the bars. So the purpose of a castle is to keep people out, and the purpose of a prison is to keep people in.

When the devil begins to build a stronghold in a person's mind, this person becomes like a prisoner behind bars. The devil has enslaved him or her in the wrong kind of thinking. And not only has he enslaved this person, but the devil has placed lies in their mind that have become so real to him or her, it is like a person who's living inside a castle. Those on the outside who can see the truth clearly and want to help, can't quite seem to get through the barrier — the strongholds. That prevents those with the truth from being able to penetrate the mind of the captive with the help that can set that person free.

But we were not left defenseless. Paul forewarned us of the enemy's strategy, but he also gave us instructions on how to combat these strongholds. Second Corinthians 10:4 and 5 continue, "(For the weapons of our warfare are not carnal, but mighty through God to the pulling down of *strong holds*;) Casting down imaginations, and every high thing that exalteth itself against the knowledge of God, and bringing into captivity every thought to the obedience of Christ." We must take charge of our thoughts and drive the devil's lies right out of our brain!

The Devil Wants To Lord Over You With His Lies

The apostle Peter also gave us insight into how the devil operates. He said, "How God anointed Jesus of Nazareth with the Holy Ghost and with power: who went about doing good, and healing all that were *oppressed* of the devil; for God was with him."

The word "oppressed" is the Greek word *katadunasteuo,* which describes *a tyrant or wicked king who is lording himself over his subjects.* Of course, a tyrant doesn't give anyone options; he tells them where they're going to live, what they're going to eat, and what they're going to do. He enslaves and tyrannizes them until they become puppets in his hands.

In light of the meaning of this word *katadunasteuo* — translated here as "oppressed" — Acts 10:38 could be interpreted: "How God anointed Jesus of Nazareth with the Holy Ghost, and power, who went about doing good and healing all who were being tyrannized by the devil."

If you take into account the five Greek words and their meanings that we've covered in this lesson, you will see that they paint a clear picture of the devil's schemes and strategies. First, the word *diabolos,* translated "devil," lets us know that the devil comes to strike the mind with lies, allegations, and insinuations, until *dia,* he penetrates the mind. The next word is "wiles," translated from the Greek word *methodeia,* which pictures the devil paving a road into the mind because he now has access. The third word is *noemata,* the word for "devices." A form of the Greek word *nous* — meaning *the mind* — *noemata* depicts the devil's plot to confuse the mind or "scramble the brain."

Fourth is the word "stronghold," which is the Greek word *ochuroma.* The word *ochuroma* pictures the devil building strongholds into the minds of his victims that enslave them and also keep out people who could possibly help stop the devil's attacks. And finally, we covered the Greek word *katadunasteuo.* This word describes the devil as a tyrant who moves into the stronghold he's built and begins to lord himself over his enslaved subjects, dictating what they can do and what they will never be able to do, what will happen to their marriage, how much money they can earn, and how sick they will be — *the devil lords himself with lies.*

On the program, Rick shares a story about a time when the devil tried to create a stronghold in *his* life.

> When I was a young boy, I got very sick in the seventh grade, and it caused me to miss about half a year of school. When I was finally able to return to school, I felt like I was behind everyone else. Particularly, everyone else understood English and mathematics. I had missed a very important period of studies so I couldn't understand what people were talking about in class, and inwardly, I just felt so stupid.

Every day when I would look into the mirror to brush my teeth, I would hear a voice speaking to me, saying, "You're stupid. You're just plain stupid." At the time, I didn't know it was the voice of the devil, but it was the devil trying to find a way into my mind. Every day he was pounding my mind with these thoughts.

I finally graduated from the seventh grade to the eighth grade. But if I didn't understand English and mathematics in the seventh grade, how was I going to understand them in the eighth grade? The entire eighth-grade year I struggled and struggled with my self-image. I really felt genuinely inferior and stupid!

And every day when I looked in that mirror, I would hear that voice speaking to me, saying, "You're such a defect. You are inferior. You're just stupid, stupid, stupid!" I heard it every single morning before I went to school, and I began to feel that I really was stupid and inferior. The devil was paving a road into my mind and beginning to form that highway into my brain to confuse me — *to really scramble my brains about who I was.*

Miraculously I graduated from the eighth grade and made my way into the ninth grade. But in the ninth grade, we were going to study algebra. *Uh-oh!* If I didn't understand math in the seventh and eighth grades, how on earth was I going to understand ninth-grade algebra? To make matters worse, the algebra teacher was so old that she had taught my father algebra in the very same room years and years earlier, and she didn't like my dad. When my dad was in the ninth grade, he smoked a pipe in the back of her class, and she *never* forgot about that.

On the first day of class, I was already nervous. I was worried, and I was feeling stupid before we even got started because, for the last two years, I had been hearing a voice tell me, "You're so stupid," over and over again. The devil was paving that road into my mind and confusing me until I was about to thoroughly believe that I really was stupid. And then the devil brought in reinforcements — first, in the form of my algebra teacher.

On the first day of class, I went in and sat at my desk — again, *so nervous* about algebra — and she began to take attendance. She called everybody by their name, and then she got to me, Ricky Renner. And when she called my name, she stopped and said, "Renner. Ricky Renner?" I said, "Yes, that's me." She replied, "Wait, is your father Ronald Renner?" I said, "Yes, ma'am, that's my father."

Immediately, she strutted from behind her desk — she always wore stilettos. She strutted from behind that desk, leaned back against it, pushed her glasses to the bottom of her nose, looked to the back of the room at me with a scowl on her face, and said, "Stupid! Stupid! Stupid! Any child of Ronald Renner is stupid, and in this class, your name is Stupid Renner." And then she continued calling attendance.

I remember sitting there feeling like I'd been assaulted, and I hadn't done anything but show up to class. Of course, this kind of behavior by a teacher wouldn't be permitted today, but back in those days, people could get away with it. Every single day that year when she called the attendance, she not once called me Ricky Renner. She always said, "Stupid Renner," and I was expected to say, "Here." If I had to ask a question that she didn't appreciate, she would say, "Would somebody else please help Stupid?" And you know how kids are; they thought it was hilarious. So "Stupid" became my new nickname.

During my ninth-grade year, when I would walk down the halls or up the stairs and people would pass me, they would say, "Hey! Hello, Stupid!" This was the devil trying to pave a road into my mind — to confuse me and build a stronghold in my mind to tell me there was something defective about me.

And because it was the ninth grade, I was required to meet with the job placement counselors. When I took my test, they met with me and said, "Ricky, we don't want to hurt your feelings, but after observing your test, we don't recommend that you ever try to go to college or university because you just don't have what is mentally required for that. It would be better for you to pave roads or dig ditches." And of course, we need people to pave roads and dig ditches, but suddenly, I was being assaulted again.

The devil was speaking to me for *two years*. Then he brought in reinforcements: a teacher who called me stupid *every day* in front of my peers; the students who found it funny until the whole school called me stupid; and the job placement counselors who told me I didn't have much of a future. I still remember sitting across the table looking at them as they basically told me that I was mentally defective, and again, it confirmed to me that I was stupid.

The devil was trying to take me down. And by the end of the ninth grade, it was like a tyrant had moved into my head, and I was being dominated by this insinuation that I was defective, inferior, and I was simply stupid. I was less than everyone else, and in fact, my future was going to be spent digging ditches and laying asphalt. That would be my destiny, which was very different from what I had hoped for earlier in my life.

I felt *so conquered*, but do you know what saved me? I got baptized in the Holy Spirit. In 1974, I received the infilling of the Holy Spirit, and the power of God came into me. And when the power of God came into me, it broke all the shackles the devil was trying to use to mentally enslave me. None of what the devil or anyone else was saying to me was true, but the devil knew if he could conquer my mind and emotions, he could take me down. But when I received the baptism in the Holy Spirit, those shackles *literally* just fell off of me, and *I walked free!*

I'm not tooting my own horn, but I think you can tell by listening to my programs or reading my books that, if anything, I'm not stupid! I'm a pretty intellectual guy, and I give God the glory for it. He has given me a wonderful brain, and I'm so thankful for it!

The devil knew that God had a future for Rick. And the devil didn't want him to step into God's plan for his life, so he tried to hijack him from the very beginning by striking his mind again and again until he found an entrance by paving a road into his head and regularly assaulting his mind and identity. He began to confuse Rick and what he believed about himself. Finally, he became so confused that a stronghold was built in his mind, and the devil moved in like a tyrant. Jesus and the Holy Spirit were in his heart, but the devil was dominating Rick's mind.

This is why it is so very important you listen to the *right* voice — the voice of the Holy Spirit — and not the voice of the enemy. And if the enemy is speaking to you, then you have to say *no* to him and open your spiritual ears to hear what the Word of God says to you. "(For the weapons of our warfare are not carnal, but mighty through God to the pulling down of strong holds;) Casting down imaginations, and every high thing that exalted itself against the knowledge of God, and bringing into captivity every thought to the obedience of Christ" (2 Corinthians 10:4,5).

STUDY QUESTIONS

Study to shew thyself approved unto God, a workman that needeth not to be ashamed, rightly dividing the word of truth.
— 2 Timothy 2:15

1. What is the devil's destination and what can you do to stop him from reaching it?
2. How does the devil operate? Give your answer using the five Greek words and meanings mentioned in this lesson.
3. Why does the devil attack the mind?

PRACTICAL APPLICATION

But be ye doers of the word, and not hearers only, deceiving your own selves.
— James 1:22

1. The devil attacks through the mind and emotions with negative thoughts and feelings. What are some ways you can recognize such an attack before the devil forms a stronghold in your mind?
2. Dealing with an attack from the devil can be difficult — especially if you're dealing with persistent negative thoughts. But there is strength in numbers. Who in your life can you call on for support and to encourage and pray with you through such an attack?

TOPIC

Telltale Signs That Bitterness Is Growing in Your Heart

Editor's Note: This lesson was taken from Rick Renner's *Sparkling Gems From the Greek, Volume 1*: September 4. *Sparkling Gems From the Greek* is a daily devotional from the Greek language of the New Testament.

SCRIPTURES

1. **Hebrews 12:14a** — Follow peace with all men, and holiness, without which no man shall see the Lord…

2. **Hebrews 12:14b** — …Without which no man shall see the Lord…

3. **Hebrews 12:15** — Looking diligently lest any man fail of the grace of God; lest any root of bitterness springing up trouble you, and thereby many be defiled.

4. **Matthew 12:34** — O generation of vipers, how can ye, being evil, speak good things? for out of the abundance of the heart the mouth speaketh.

GREEK WORDS

1. "follow" — **διώκω** (*dioko*): to follow closely; an old hunting term which means to hunt; pictures a hunter who is dressed in hunting clothes, prepared with hunting gear, and is determined to follow the tracks of the animal being hunted until it is captured

2. "looking diligently" — **ἐπισκοπος** (*episkopos*): where we get the word for the Episcopalian church; a compound of the words **ἐπί** (*epi*) and **σκοπος** (*skopos*); the word **ἐπί** (*epi*) means over, and the word **σκοπος** (*skopos*) means to look; compounded, **ἐπισκοπος** (*episkopos*) describes intensely looking at something; it's where we get the words "microscope" and "telescope"; can also be translated as "bishop," as in "bishoping" oneself

3. "root of bitterness" — πικρία (*pikria*): the word for "bitterness" describes something that is deeply rooted, not superficial, and is something that is caustic, bitter, or sour

4. "trouble" — ἐνοχλέω (*enochleo*): to harass; to torment; describes someone who bothers, upsets, or haunts

5. "defiled" — μιαίνω (*miaino*): to spot or stain

6. "springing up" — φύω (*phuo*): describes a small plant that begins to poke up through the soil

SYNOPSIS

Roots of bitterness in your heart can jeopardize your own happiness and peace. The Lord has a perfect plan for your life, full of blessings and grace to do what He has purposed you to do. But if you are constantly wrestling with grudges and roots of bitterness, you run the risk of frustrating the grace of God on your life. You alone are responsible for your heart. The Bible says not only do roots of bitterness affect your peace, but they defile the people around you. Don't give place to bitterness — give way to the grace of God.

The emphasis of this lesson:

The Bible tells us in Hebrews 12:15, "Looking diligently lest any man fail of the grace of God; lest any root of bitterness springing up trouble you, and thereby many be defiled." The phrase, "looking diligently" can be translated in the Greek, in some form, as *bishop* and can refer to *"bishoping" oneself*. You have the responsibility to look after the state of your own heart. You must humble yourself and follow peace to stay in the grace of God for your life.

Follow Peace With All Men

What are the telltale signs that bitterness is growing in your heart? The Bible tells us in Hebrews:

> **Follow peace with all men, and holiness, without which no man shall see the Lord...**
>
> **— Hebrews 12:14**

Notice the word "follow." The word "follow" is the Greek word *dioko* — an old hunting term that means *to hunt*. It pictures *a hunter who has put on his hunting clothes, has his hunting gear and weapon, and he's determined to follow the tracks of the animal he's hunting. He's going to follow the scent of that animal, and he's not going to stop until he finally captures his prey.* That is the word used in Hebrews 12:14.

The Greek form of *dioko* in this verse means *to follow and keep on following peace with all men.* That means that oftentimes, peace doesn't come to you; you have to develop a strategy to find peace with all men. You must follow the tracks of peace, and sometimes those tracks are hard to find. You have to look for every "broken branch" and follow the "scent" of peace. You must determine in your heart, *I'm not going to finish until I finally capture what the Bible calls, "Peace with all men"* (*see* Hebrews 12:14). The word "all" is all-encompassing, and it really does mean *all men.* In fact, the verse goes on to say, "...Without which no man shall see the Lord."

Wow! What does that mean, "...No man *shall see* the Lord"? Does that mean you're going to lose your salvation if you don't have peace with all men? No, it doesn't mean that. The words "shall see" mean if a person pursues peace with others, *he or she will not be admitted into the immediate presence of God.* In other words, if you have strife in your life that is working in place of peace, it becomes a blocker that causes you to no longer experience the presence of God.

For example, if you have strife in your heart, you might go to church and feel that everyone around you is blessed, but you feel nothing. Do you know why? Because strife is a blocker — it keeps you from being admitted into the wonderful presence of the Lord. But the writer of Hebrews says that we have to be determined that we're going to follow peace with all people to the best of our ability — until we *capture* it!

The following is a testimony from Rick Renner about a time when he had to determine in his heart to follow peace until he captured it:

> When my family and I first moved to the former Soviet Union more than three decades ago, we began our church in Riga, Latvia, and we were on television. Because we were on television, our church began to grow very rapidly.
>
> There happened to be another pastor in our town who was not very happy about our church's rapid growth. And, in fact, he had declared that his church was the only church worth attending. His church was the church of the city until that time, and when

our church began to grow, he began to be very upset with me because he felt I was usurping his place.

One day, he stood in the pulpit of his church and said, "Well, there's another pastor in town — a new guy. I don't want to say his name, but he's bald," and he said, "I just want to tell you, *Don't go to that church, because anyone who is bald is under a curse.*"

When I first heard of this, I laughed out loud. I started losing my hair when I was 17 years old. I don't know life with hair; I've always looked like this as long as I can remember.

At first, I thought what that pastor said was funny, but then it really began to get under my skin that this man would be so carnal as to say I was cursed because I was bald! If that was the only reason he could find to tell people not to come to my church, that was ridiculous! But what he said began to penetrate so deep that I became perturbed with him. He kept saying bad things about me, and I kept hearing more and more of those bad things he was saying.

Then I found myself doing something just as ugly as what he had been doing. He was a short guy, so one day, I said, "Listen, there's another man in town who says that anybody who is bald is under a curse. But in my opinion, anybody is cursed who is a midget like him. *He's* obviously the one who's cursed!"

It came out of my mouth, and as soon as it did, I saw Denise sitting in the front row saying, "*Ugh!* Rick, *why did you say that?*" But I said it, and it launched an all-out war between me and that pastor.

And it got worse. There was mudslinging and bickering back and forth between the two churches. One day, the Lord spoke to me and said, *Rick, do you want revival in your lif*e? I said, "Lord, You know I want revival in my life."

And He asked me a second time, *Do you want revival in your life?* Again, I said, "Lord, You know I want revival in my life." He replied, *If you really want revival in your life, you need to go to that man, and you need to get on your knees and apologize to him for your attitude and for the things you've said about him.*

And I heard the Lord say again, *Do you want revival in your life?*
But this time, I said, "Lord, I'm not so sure." If I had to go to
that pastor and get on my knees, I didn't know if I really wanted
a revival that badly. But you know, sometimes the Holy Spirit is
like the Hound of Heaven; He just stays on your tail until, finally,
you do what He's telling you to do!

Every day, I would hear the Lord say over and over again, *Are you
going to obey Me?* And, finally, I said, "Yes, I'm going to obey You!"
Before I knew it, I was in my car driving to the other side of the
city. When I walked into that other pastor's building, people were
stunned that I had entered the premises because they knew I was
the "big enemy" from the other side of the city.

I went up a couple of flights of stairs, down a long hallway, and
walked into his office. When I walked in, he was so shocked that
I was there. I said, "I've come to talk to you today." I sat across
the table from him and kept thinking, *Get on my knees? Get on my
knees? You've got to be kidding. Do I have to get on my knees?* But I
knew what I had been told to do.

But rather than do it quickly, we talked about the weather, we
talked about our kids, we talked about politics — we talked about
so many things. And when there was nothing left to talk about,
I knew it was my moment. So I dropped down on one knee and
looked up into his face. I could see he was so happy to see me on
my knees, and I kept thinking, *You're the one who ought to be on
your knees!* But I was the one the Lord told to get on his knees.
I was there because God was dealing with *my* attitude. I was on
that one knee when I *literally* heard the Holy Spirit say, "Both
knees!"

So I dropped onto my second knee, looked across the pastor's
desk, and said, "I am here today to apologize to you for things I
have heard about you that I entertained, and for things I have said
about you." This was a very difficult thing for me to do because he
had said some really bad things about me. He started this whole
thing, but I engaged it. I entered into the fray with him. And now
the Holy Spirit was dealing with me.

When I got up from my knees, I began on a new trek to pursue
peace with this pastor. I'm telling you, I had to really pursue it —

I had to decide to follow it over and over again. And, eventually, I captured peace with this man. That was many, many years ago — and to this day, he is a very dear friend of mine.

But it didn't begin that way. I really love this man today, and although I don't agree with everything he does, I really appreciate the many sacrifices that he has made for the Gospel.

Removing Strife From Your Life

If you want to have peace with all men and experience revival and the presence of God in your life, you *must* remove strife. In the book of Hebrews, the writer talks about a root of bitterness that can grow and spread larger and larger in your life if you fail in this area of "pursuing peace."

Looking diligently lest any man fail of the grace of God; lest any root of bitterness springing up trouble you, and thereby many be defiled.

— Hebrews 12:15

Notice how verse 15 begins. It says, "…Looking diligently…." The phrase "looking diligently" is an interesting translation of the Greek word *episkopos*, which is where we get the word for the Episcopalian church. It's the compound of the words *epi* and *skopos*. The word *epi* means *over*, and the word *skopos* means *to look* — and it's where we get the words "microscope" and "telescope." It describes *looking very intensely at something*, but when you compound it with the word *epi*, it forms the word *episkopos*, which is also translated in the New Testament as the word "bishop." You could actually translate *episkopos* as *bishoping yourself.*

This phrase "bishoping yourself" means every person is a bishop. You may be thinking, *A bishop of what?* You are a bishop *of your own heart.* It is your heart, and God gave you responsibility for your heart. The buck stops with you when it comes to your heart. Even if someone else has wronged you, God will hold *you* responsible for what you have allowed to fester in your heart. God has given you oversight over your heart. You're the one who has to say *yes* or *no* to unforgiveness and bitterness — ***you are responsible for your heart.*** If you translate the first part of Hebrews 12:15 using the Greek translation of "looking diligently," you find that it really means *to take care of your heart diligently.*

You have to be serious about keeping your heart in good shape.

Don't 'Fail of the Grace of God'

Hebrews 12:15 says, "Looking diligently lest any man fail of the grace of God…." But *how in the world do you fail of the grace of God?* Grace is something that God freely gives to us, and yet you can fail of the grace of God. In fact, the apostle Paul says you can *frustrate* the grace of God (*see* Galatians 2:21). When God's grace comes, it empowers you to do what you could never do by yourself. For example, when the Lord told Rick to go to that rival pastor and to get on his knees and repent, the grace of God came on him to do it. Grace empowered him to do what the Lord told him to do. Even though it was difficult, the grace of God empowered him to do what he needed to do to have peace with that man.

Rick could have frustrated the grace of God. He could have said, "Yes, Lord. I know that's what You're telling me to do, but I'm not going to do it." You have to *cooperate* with the grace of God. If you don't cooperate with it, you'll frustrate it, and you can fail of the grace that was provided to help you do the difficult thing you were tasked to do. In particular, when it comes to relationships, a sudden grace may come upon you to ask for forgiveness. But if you resist the grace of God to do it, you can frustrate the grace of God, and as a result, you can fail of the grace of God. In other words, the grace can't do what it was sent to do because of your failure to cooperate. Or you can say, "I'm going to embrace the grace" and do what you have to do to have peace with all men.

But if you fail of the grace of God, the Bible details what will happen to you. Again, Hebrews 12:15 reads:

> **Looking diligently lest any man fail of the grace of God; lest any root of bitterness springing up trouble you, and thereby many be defiled.**

This verse talks about a "root of bitterness." The word "bitterness" is the Greek word *pikria*. It describes something that is *deeply rooted, not superficial*. This word describes *that which is caustic, bitter, sour, sharp, and very deep-rooted*.

For example, you may have something against someone you've never even met because someone in your family had a problem with him or her. That root of bitterness passed from your family member all the way into you.

Roots of bitterness even can go from one generation to the next generation. *Wow, that is powerful!*

You can always tell you have a root of bitterness if you have a sarcastic attitude about someone. And the Bible explains that if you'll pay attention, you will notice when a root of bitterness begins to grow. Verse 15 says, "…Lest any root of bitterness springing up…." The word for "springing up" is the Greek word *phuo*, which describes *a small plant that begins to poke up through the soil.* It doesn't grow up overnight, but little by little, it begins to form a root system and then peek through the ground and grow.

If you begin to see bitterness in your life, it is evidence that there are roots deep down that are producing that bitter growth, and those roots need to be dealt with. Hebrews 12:15 goes on to say, "…Lest any root of bitterness springing up trouble you, and thereby many be defiled." The word "trouble" is the Greek word *enochleo*, which means *to harass or torment.* It describes *someone who follows you, haunting you and staying on your trail at all times.* It is tormenting. And here we find that when a root of bitterness is working in you, thoughts of the person that you are bitter toward will haunt you. They will hound and harass you, and your thoughts will be constantly harassing thoughts.

If you see that person being blessed, you won't be able to be blessed at their blessing. You'll just be hounded by the things going on in their life. The Bible says if you don't deal with bitterness, eventually many will be defiled (*see* Hebrews 12:15). The word "defiled" is from a form of the Greek word *miaino*, which means *to spot* or *stain.* For example, if you're walking across a white carpet and you accidentally trip and spill a glass of juice on the carpet, what does it do? It stains the carpet — and every time you walk by that stain, you're reminded of that moment when you made the spill.

Here's what happens when a root of bitterness is troubling you — it will affect your speech! Bitter people will begin to talk to others, and those people will likely talk to others. That's how the root system spreads, and that's how many become defiled.

Jesus clearly said, "…Out of the abundance of the heart the mouth speaketh" (*see* Matthew 12:34). *What is inside you is going to come out.* So if you have bitterness inside you, eventually, you're going to begin speaking your bitterness about the people you don't like. And the words you speak will begin to spot and stain those who are listening to you. Perhaps they didn't have a bad opinion of that person, but by the time you're finished speaking badly about him or her and voicing all your bitterness — in the mind of the listeners — that person will never be seen the same way again.

When you open your mouth and begin to spread bitterness that you've allowed in your heart, you *spot*, *stain*, and *contaminate* the minds of others. When you do that, not only will your bitterness hound and stalk you, but it will spot and stain the people surrounding you. That's why Rick and Denise made a decision when their sons were young that if they ever had a bad experience with anyone in the ministry or in their church, *they would never discuss it in front of their kids.*

This is a mistake many adults make with their children. Many pastors have made the mistake of freely talking in front of their children about people who have hurt them, and their children personalized that. They felt it very deeply, and it nearly destroyed them because it fostered bitterness in them that they carried into adulthood.

You need to be careful about what you say. Don't give bitterness you may be harboring to someone else and defile them, especially your own children or grandchildren. Make sure your children think the church is the most happy place in the world. They're going to wake up one day and have their own bad experiences, so don't give them yours. Instead, you need to embrace the grace of God, so it can empower you to make everything right.

STUDY QUESTIONS

Study to shew thyself approved unto God, a workman that needeth not to be ashamed, rightly dividing the word of truth.
— 2 Timothy 2:15

1. What is the Greek word and definition for the word "trouble," and how does it correlate to what roots of bitterness do in our lives?
2. What did the apostle Paul mean when he wrote "…and thereby many be defiled…" in Hebrews 12:15?
3. What do you have to do to have peace with all men and experience revival in your life? How does the Greek word that means *to hunt* relate to the quest for peace?

PRACTICAL APPLICATION

**But be ye doers of the word, and not hearers only,
deceiving your own selves.
— James 1:22**

1. Who or what do you most often find yourself becoming bitter toward
    or talking and thinking badly about? What can you do to change your
    way of thinking about this person or thing?

2. Have you ever had roots of bitterness steal your joy, peace, and bless-
    ings, and you *knew* it was because of your attitude? What can you do
    to extract those roots and prevent this from happening again?

3. Reflect on ways you can be responsible for your own heart, such as
    spending extra time in prayer, journaling, and seeking godly counsel.

LESSON 5

TOPIC

What Is a Cloud of Witnesses?

Editor's Note: This lesson was taken from Rick Renner's *Sparkling Gems
From the Greek, Volume 1*: February 17. *Sparkling Gems From the Greek* is a
daily devotional from the Greek language of the New Testament.

SCRIPTURES

1. **Hebrews 11:6** — But without faith it is impossible to please him....

2. **Hebrews 12:1** — Wherefore seeing we also are compassed about with
    so great a cloud of witnesses, let us lay aside every weight, and the sin
    which doth so easily beset us, and let us run with patience the race
    that is set before us.

3. **Hebrews 12:2** — Looking unto Jesus the author and finisher of our
    faith; who for the joy that was set before him endured the cross, despis-
    ing the shame, and is set down at the right hand of the throne of God.

GREEK WORDS

1. "without" — **χωρὶς** (*choris*): to be outside of something, such as someone who lives outside the perimeters of a city; here, to be outside of faith; describes faith as an address or an assignment

2. "compassed" — **περίκειμαι** (*perikeimai*): compound of the Greek words **περί** (*peri*) and **κεῖμαι** (*keimai*); the word **περί** (*peri*) means around and describes a circle, as something all around you; the word **κεῖμαι** (*keimai*) means to be stacked high; compounded, it portrays the idea of being completely encircled by something on every side; to lift up your eyes and look around

3. "cloud" — **νέφος** (*nephos*): a cloud

4. "witnesses" — **μαρτύρων** (*martyron*): first-hand knowledge; a factual and dependable account; where we get the word martyr

5. "lay aside" — **ἀποτίθημι** (*apotithemi*): compound of the Greek words **ἀπό** (*apo*) and **τίθημι** (*tithemi*); the word **ἀπό** (*apo*) means away and off; the word **τίθημι** (*tithemi*) means to place or position; compounded, describes a person who disrobes at the end of the day and, **ἀπό** (*apo*), pushes them so far away that he can't easily reach over to pick them up and put them back on again

6. "weight" — **ὄγκος** (*ogkos*): describes anything that weighs something down or is a hindrance

7. "which doth so easily beset us" — **εὐπερίστατος** (*euperistatos*): a triple compound of the Greek words (*eu*), (*peri*), and (*statos*); (*eu*) describes something easy, good, or comfortable; (*peri*) describes what is around you; your surroundings; and (*statos*) describes something that is standing; compounded, means the sin which stands around us; describes an environment that is comfortable, but it is the wrong environment

8. "run" — **τρέχω** (*trecho*): to move one's feet as fast as one can move them; to run so fast that one's feet never hit the ground

9. "race" — **ἀγών** (*agon*): refers to athletic conflicts and competitions that were famous in the ancient world; pictures a wrestling match

SYNOPSIS

Hebrews 12:1 and 2 tell us that we have a race of faith set before us, but it also encourages us that we are "compassed about with so great a cloud of witnesses…," and have the perfect example in Jesus, "the author and finisher of our faith." Not only can we finish this race of faith, but we can finish it victoriously!

The emphasis of this lesson:

Sometimes walking out the will of God can be tricky. Your flesh tries to wrestle with you, and you can often be tempted to stay in a comfortable environment that you're familiar with, but it won't help you to fulfill God's plan for your life or grow your faith. But the good news is that you have a perfect example of how to finish your race of faith in Jesus! By His example, you can run and finish your race of faith with confidence because you know He has already run the race of faith and was victorious!

The Heroes of Faith

The Bible provides great insight and encouragement on how we are to run our spiritual race. Hebrews 12:1 and 2 says, "Wherefore seeing we also are compassed about with so great a cloud of witnesses, let us lay aside every weight, and the sin which doth so easily beset us, and let us run with patience the race that is set before us, looking unto Jesus the author and finisher of our faith; who for the joy that was set before him endured the cross, despising the shame, and is set down at the right hand of the throne of God."

To fully understand Hebrews 12:1 and 2, we must begin in Hebrews 11 where the Bible talks about the heroes of faith — men and women who received a Word from God and did not waver from it. These "heroes of faith" were just normal people — like you and me — who got a Word from God and made the decision to stand by that promise and never let loose of it until they saw its manifestation. They stood firm in their faith that God would deliver on His promise!

Faith is an essential part of our relationship with God. Hebrews 11:6 says, "But *without* faith it is impossible to please him…." The word "without" is the Greek word *choris* and it means *to be outside of something, such as someone who lives outside the perimeters of a city.* Here, the word "without" indicates being outside of *faith*, and it describes *faith as an address* or *assignment.* When God gives you a word — a promise — you are to stay *in* a place of faith and not let go of it. And the Word says that when you stay in that place of faith, it pleases Him.

With that in mind, let's look at Hebrews 12:1.

Wherefore seeing we also are compassed about with so great a cloud of witnesses, let us lay aside every weight, and the sin which doth so easily beset us, and let us run with patience the race that is set before us.

Notice this verse begins, "Wherefore seeing we also are *compassed* about…." The word "compassed" is a translation from the Greek word *perikeimai*. It is a compound of the words *peri*, meaning *around*, and *keimai*, meaning *to be stacked*. This word *perikeimai* — translated as "compassed" in Hebrews 12:1, literally means *to lift up your eyes and look*. All around the faithful ones — abounding on every side — were witnesses. Those who received a Word from God, and because they had faith and stayed with that Word, *saw the manifestation of this great cloud of witnesses*.

A Cloud of Witnesses

There are many examples of people who have received a Word from God and had the faith to see it through. Hebrews 12:1 continues, "…We also are compassed about with so great a *cloud* of witnesses." The word "cloud" is the Greek word *nephos* and it can be translated as *a cloud*, but what does "a cloud of witnesses" mean?

Some people like to imagine "a cloud of witnesses" as a cloud filled with witnesses floating across the sky. However, that's not what it means. This is an example of having to dive *deep* into the text to understand its meaning. This word "cloud," translated from the Greek word *nephos* that is used in the context of Hebrews 12:1, was very specifically used to describe *the highest seats in a stadium or amphitheater*.

For example, if you wanted to get good seats to a show or performance, you would get there early because stadiums tend to fill up very quickly. And if you were late to the show, you would have to buy tickets for whatever seats were still available. The ticket salesman would tell you that the only seats left were the seats in the *nephos* or *seats in the clouds*. Why is this important? Because Hebrews 12:1 says, "Lift up your eyes and look! You're surrounded on every side by witnesses — all the way to the highest seats in the clouds. *You're surrounded by a cloud of witnesses!*"

This is important because if you're surrounded by a stadium filled with people who have already walked in faith and seen the manifestation of it, it means *you* are on the playing field. That's why you can look up to the top of the stands because *you are on the playing field!* These witnesses have already played their game and won, so now they're sitting in the stands and cheering you on because it's your time to run your race of faith! You are on the playing field, but if you lift up your eyes you will see that you're surrounded by the "cloud of witnesses" from Hebrews 11 and so many others who have run their race before you!

You Have To Die to Some Things To Walk Out His Plan

Again, Hebrews 12:1 says, "Wherefore seeing we also are compassed about with so great a cloud of witnesses...." In the original Greek, it's actually translated "... With *such* a great cloud of witnesses...." It is describing the *quality* of the people in the stands — people who ran their race of faith, did what God called them to do, and are now cheering us on.

Notice the Bible calls them "a great cloud of *witnesses*." The word "witnesses" is a form of the Greek word *martyron*. This word *martyron* is where we get the word "martyr," which means *sometimes you have to die to some things in order to walk out the will of God*. This word describes having to die to the flesh, your own desires, and the opinions of others.

Hebrews 12:1 goes on to say:

> **...Let us *lay aside* every weight, and the sin which doth so easily beset us, and let us run with patience the race that is set before us.**

The words "lay aside" are a translation of the Greek word *apotithemi*, which is a compound of the preposition *apo*, which means *away*, and *tithemi*, which means *to place or position*. But when you put these two words together, they form *apotithemi*, which describes *a person who disrobes at the end of the day*. It pictures a person who comes home after a long day and says, "I've worn these clothes all day and they're no longer fitting for me." Maybe they're dirty or not appropriate to go to sleep in, so he disrobes and lays them aside. And because the preposition *apo* is added to this root word, it means this person does not just remove his clothes, he pushes them so far away from himself that he can't easily reach over to pick them up and put them back on again.

From this word *apotithemi*, we get a picture of a deliberate decision to remove anything that hinders us and push it so *far away* that we can't revert to it again — we're deliberately removing it from our life. This lets us know that if we're going to run our race victoriously, there are some things we have to remove and push far away from us. But what things do we have to remove?

Hebrews 12:1 gives us the answer. It says that we are to "lay aside every weight...." The word "weight," the Greek word *ogkos*, describes *anything that weighs you down or is a hindrance*. This "hindrance" may be a habit or even a wrong way of thinking.

The verse continues, "Let us lay aside every weight, and the sin *which doth so easily beset us*...." But what is a "sin which doth so easily beset us?" These words are translated from the Greek word *euperistatos*, which is a triple compound of the words *eu*, *peri*, and *statos*. The preposition *eu* describes *something easy, good*, or *comfortable*. The word *peri* describes *what is around you*. Lastly, the word *statos* describes *something that is standing*. When compounded, these three words form *euperistatos*, which means *the sin that stands around us*, or *the sin that so easily environs us*. It describes an environment that is easy and comfortable, but it's *the wrong environment*.

This wrong environment may be an environment in which you feel comfortable because you've been there for a long time. For example, maybe you're going to a church that doesn't encourage your faith, but you've been attending services there for many years. So you may be comfortable in this environment, even though your faith won't grow if you remain in it. Or maybe you have a particular group of friends who have been your friends for a very long time. You're comfortable around them and you love them, but these friends have a way of bringing you down.

Hebrews 12:1 exhorts you to lay aside the environment that seems so casual and comfortable to you, but it may not be a positive environment for the development of your faith. You need to be very careful about who you call "friends" because you want to make sure you're living in the right environment.

Another example is if you smoke or drink or have some other kind of habit that you tend to do only when you're with a particular group of people. You may need to take a break from that kind of environment. This verse encourages you to choose a new group of friends, attend a new church, or take a break from whatever environment is hindering you from growing your faith.

Hebrews 12:1 concludes:

...And let us _run_ with patience the _race_ that is set before us.

In the Greek text, it seems there's a confusion of metaphors. There's the word "run," the Greek word _trecho_, and it means _to move your feet as fast as you can move them_. It depicts _a person running so fast that their feet never hit the ground_. Then we see the word "race." "Race" is the Greek word _agon_, which is actually the word for _a wrestling match_.

But when we look at the meanings of these two Greek words within the context of Hebrews 12:1, we get a powerful visual image. When you begin to run your race of faith, you may experience a wrestling in your soul. Your soul may say, _Wow, this is really hard!_ Your soul may try to fight you at every turn, yet you're commanded to run your race of faith.

The good news is, the Bible says to "run with patience the race that is set before us," which means we don't need to have everything figured out — _the race has already been pre-planned by the Lord!_

When Rick and Denise first got married, Rick decided that he was going to start jogging every night. He ran between two to five miles at 10:00 p.m. every single night. Rick had never run before, so it was all new for him. Fortunately, a friend of his said, "Rick, don't worry about it. Don't worry about where you're going to run or how far you're going to run. I will plan the route, and we will run together." So Rick just ran alongside his friend. Rick went everywhere he told him to go. If his friend turned left, so did Rick. If he went straight, so did Rick. If he went around the block, Rick went around the block. _Rick didn't have to think about the route or how far or fast to go because his friend had already planned it for him._

In the same way, when you begin your race of faith, you don't have to understand everything — you just have to run with the Lord and do what He tells you to do.

Another example of how to run our race of faith is found in the ancient stadium in Anatolia or Asia Minor. This stadium in the city of Aphrodisias is 2,000 years old, and it's very well preserved. When the runners ran their races in this ancient stadium, they didn't have to figure out where to run; all they had to do was get into the stadium and start running because the racetrack was already prepared. And in this same way, _God has a plan prepared for you._

Jesus, the Author and Finisher

There is great comfort in the fact that God has a plan for you. All He needs from you is your willingness to say *yes*. And when your flesh tries to argue, you have to make the decision to say *no* to your flesh and say, "Jesus, I'm going to keep running with you." And the inspiration and motivation to keep running is found in the next verse. Hebrews 12:2 says:

> **Looking unto Jesus the author and finisher of *our* faith; who for the joy that was set before him endured the cross, despising the shame, and is set down at the right hand of the throne of God.**

The word "our" was inserted (and italicized) by the writers of the *New King James Version* Bible. The Greek translation did not include the word "our." It says, "Looking unto Jesus the author and finisher of faith." From this we see an example of Jesus — He started His race and He finished His race *of faith!*

Many people start off their race strong, but they end with a disappointing fizzle — *they don't follow through*. Don't let that be your story. You may not know how to get to where you're going, but at least you need to know where you're headed — toward Jesus! That's why Hebrews 12:2 exhorts us to keep "Looking unto Jesus the author and finisher of our faith...." *Jesus is to be our example of starting and finishing*. And the verse goes on to say, "...Who for the joy that was set before him endured the cross...." That is Jesus' example of wrestling with the flesh.

You have to make Jesus your example. He began His race and dealt with a lot of flak along the way from naysayers and religious people who tried to belittle Him and take Him down, but Jesus kept His eyes on the prize. And the prize for Jesus was being exalted at the right hand of the Father and pouring out the gift of the Holy Spirit and the birth of the church — *this* is what Jesus had on His mind. This was the joy that was set before Him, and *He wasn't going to let it go*! Jesus never took His eyes off His goal.

Likewise, when *you* run your race of faith, you have to remember there's a goal in front of you. You must determine to finish and do what God has asked you to do. If you start to feel discouraged, just look to Jesus as the ultimate example of one who started His race and finished it well.

Don't begin with a bang and end with a fizzle! Go all the way to the end until you can say, "I have done what the Lord has asked me to do." Just

look around you! You are *surrounded* by people who have already done
it — *a cloud of witnesses* — and they are cheering you on to victory!

STUDY QUESTIONS

**Study to shew thyself approved unto God, a workman that
needeth not to be ashamed, rightly dividing the word of truth.
— 2 Timothy 2:15**

1. What example did Jesus set for us in Hebrews 12:2 as we run our race
    of faith?
2. In your own words, what is "a cloud of witnesses"?
3. According to Hebrews 12:1, what do you need to die to or remove
    from your life in order to walk out the will of God?

PRACTICAL APPLICATION

**But be ye doers of the word, and not hearers only,
deceiving your own selves.
—James 1:22**

1. What does "a cloud of witnesses" mean for you? How does this visual
    encourage you in your walk of faith?
2. Think about your habits and environments. Can you think of any you
    need to die to or remove from your life?
3. Have you ever been tempted to let go of a Word you've received from
    God? How can you encourage yourself to finish your race of faith
    and walk out the will of God with confidence? Write them down and
    meditate on them for future reference.

TOPIC

On What Basis Will You Be Rewarded?

Editor's Note: This lesson was taken from Rick Renner's *Sparkling Gems From the Greek, Volume 2:* March 2 – March 3. *Sparkling Gems From the Greek* is a daily devotional from the Greek language of the New Testament.

SCRIPTURES

1. **1 Corinthians 3:11** — For other foundation can no man lay than that is laid, which is Jesus Christ.

2. **1 Corinthians 3:12-15** — Now if any man build upon this foundation gold, silver, precious stones, wood, hay, stubble; every man's work shall be made manifest: for the day shall declare it, because it shall be revealed by fire; and the fire shall try every man's work of what sort it is. If any man's work abide which he hath built thereupon, he shall receive a reward. If any man's work shall be burned, he shall suffer loss: but he himself shall be saved; yet so as by fire.

GREEK WORDS

1. "every man" — εκαστος (*hekastos*): an all-inclusive term that embraces everyone, with no one excluded

2. "revealed" — αποκαλυπτω (*apokalupto*): to uncover, reveal, or unveil; something that has been veiled or hidden but then suddenly becomes clear and visible to the mind or eye; a sudden revealing; when the veil is removed and what was hidden comes into plain view; when what is behind a veil is no longer concealed or hidden from private or public view

3. "abide" — μενω (*meno*): to stay, dwell, lodge, remain, or continue

Many believers are familiar with the phrase "a wise man builds his house on the rock," but what does this really mean? The Bible talks a lot about the foundations you should build your life on, and in this lesson, Rick focuses on First Corinthians 3:11-15 and explains exactly how the Bible says you should build your life and what you should build your life with.

The emphasis of this lesson:

In this lesson, you will learn how to build your life in a way that will last and in a way that will be rewarded. It is easy to assume that our reward in Heaven will correlate with the number of accomplishments we have achieved on the earth, but the Bible clearly states our reward comes from the *quality* of our life and what we have used to build it. Everyone's work will be tested by the fires of life, and those who have built their lives on the foundation of Jesus Christ — those who have built their lives to last — will be rewarded.

Jesus Christ, the Foundation of Our Lives

Many people think they will be rewarded for accomplishing a lot of things in their lives. But what does the Bible say about the basis on which we will be rewarded? To answer this question, we must begin in First Corinthians where the apostle Paul wrote to the Church of Corinth. It says:

> **For other foundation can no man lay than that is laid, which is Jesus Christ.**
>
> **— 1 Corinthians 3:11**

In this verse, Paul said the only way we can begin a Christian life is by building our life on the foundation of Jesus Christ and His Lordship. But that is simply the place to begin. The passage goes on to say:

> **Now if any man build upon this foundation gold, silver, precious stones, wood, hay, stubble; Every man's work shall be made manifest: for the day shall declare it, because it shall be revealed by fire; and the fire shall try every man's work of what sort it is. If any man's work abide which he hath built thereupon, he shall receive a reward. If any man's work shall be**

burned, he shall suffer loss: but he himself shall be saved; yet so as by fire.

— 1 Corinthians 3:12-15

These are amazing verses, and as we take a closer look at what Paul said, we will understand on what basis we're going to be rewarded in Heaven one day. Let's circle back to verse 11, where Paul said:

For other foundation can no man lay than that is laid, which is Jesus Christ.

There is your foundation. Jesus Christ is the starting point of your Christian life — He is your foundation — but you have a great responsibility for what you build on top of that foundation. That is why Paul continued in verse 12, saying:

Now if any man builds upon this foundation gold, silver, precious stones, wood, hay, stubble; Every man's work shall be made manifest: for the day shall declare it, because it shall be revealed by fire…

— 1 Corinthians 3:12,13

Built To Last

What in the world was Paul talking about? In the ancient world, buildings were built out of each of the materials listed in verse 12 — precious stone, wood, hay, and stubble. For example, the imperial buildings in the city of Rome were constructed of granite — some of it was brought all the way from Aswan, Egypt — and beautiful marble and marble veneers that were decked out with precious gems.

But scattered among these beautiful buildings were also shanties where the slaves lived. Every slave lived in this kind of little home, which was a hut made of wood, hay, and stubble. And these shanties were what Paul was referring to in verse 12.

From time to time, fires would be ignited in these ancient cities, and because all the slave homes were made of wood, hay, and stubble, they burned up quickly in a puff of smoke. The embers would be carried throughout the city in the air, and one little shanty would ignite another and another until the whole city was on fire.

The fire would burn from one side of the city all the way to the other. Finally, when the blaze was gone and the fire was out, everything that had been constructed of wood, hay, and stubble was gone. The *only thing* that remained standing were the buildings that were constructed of stone. Only the stone could endure the fire.

If you read First Corinthians 3:11 in the context of these ancient cities, you will understand precisely what Paul was asking those early believers. He said, "What are you building with your life? How are you building your family? How are you building your finances? And if you're in the ministry, how are you building your ministry or church?"

But Paul wasn't referring to the physical materials people were using to build their lives; he was referring to the *quality*. Are you doing things hastily with no thought? Are you just throwing up a hut made of wood, hay, and stubble, or are you building your family, finances, relationships, business, ministry, or church to withstand and endure every test that will come along in life? These are very important questions for you to ask yourself as you build your life on the foundation of Jesus Christ.

Revealed by Fire

It is a fact that the fires of life will come to each of us, but that doesn't mean God sends the fires. Trials are just part of this world we live in. From time to time, something difficult or trying will occur in your life, and it will in turn reveal what you have built. You'll find out in that moment of crisis exactly how you've built your marriage, your finances, your ministry, your church, or what you've invested into your children. That is why Paul wrote in First Corinthians 3:13: "Every man's work shall be made manifest...."

The words "every man" in this verse are the Greek word *hekastos*, which can be translated as *every single man without exception*. This means every single man, without exception, will come to a moment when what he has built will become manifest. The Greek literally means each man's work *will become visible*. Why? The end of the verse tells us: "...Because it shall be revealed by fire...."

Again, this is not a fire sent by the Lord. It might be a fire sent by the enemy, a fire that simply comes from living in a broken world, or it might be a fire you created for yourself by some wrong decision or action. But regardless of where they come from, those fires are going to reveal what you've been building with your life.

The word "revealed" in verse 13 is the Greek word *apokalupto*, and it means *to pull back the curtains to uncover or unveil what has been hidden.* This tells us that on that day when a fire enters your life, the curtains will be pulled back to uncover what has been hidden in your life. You're going to understand what you've done right and what you've done wrong in the way you have been building every area of your life. And if you've built your life wisely and carefully — if you've built everything in your life out of stone — then what you have built will last. It will show that you have been thinking long-term instead of acting hastily. It will testify that you have decided, "No, I'm going to do things right." And if that is the case, then *no fire of life will ever affect what you've built.*

But if you have built the things in your life out of wood, hay, and stubble, they will go up in a puff of smoke and you will have to begin again. This is precisely what Paul taught in First Corinthians 3:13 — the fires of life will try every man's work and reveal the quality of what he's been building. *What a sparkling gem!*

You Will Be Rewarded

When we read verse 14, we find out the basis on which we are going to be rewarded. It says:

If any man's work abide which he hath built thereupon....
— 1 Corinthians 3:14

To review what we have learned so far from First Corinthians 3, our foundation is Jesus. But once we stand on that foundation, God gives us the responsibility and will hold us accountable for what we build on top of that rock-solid foundation. Our foundation cannot be improved, but what we do after the foundation has been laid in our life depends largely on us.

Verse 14 continues, "If any man's work abide which he hath built thereupon, he shall receive a reward." The word "reward" really describes *a payday*, meaning God will compensate you for what you have done and reward you for building the things in your life right. If your work abides — which means that when the fire comes and goes your work is still standing — *that is what you're going to be rewarded for!*

You won't be rewarded for doing a lot of activity or simply producing a large quantity of work. First Corinthians 3:14 clearly states that if any man's work *remains* and withstands the test of fire, *he will receive a reward!*

If any man's work shall be burned, he shall suffer loss: but he himself shall be saved; yet so as by fire.

— 1 Corinthians 3:15

In this verse we have a tragic picture, but at the same time, a hopeful one. If a fire comes and reveals that you have built upon the foundation of your life badly, the Lord will give you the power to restore it.

If a fire reveals that you haven't led your church correctly, or you haven't invested in your children wisely, and everything just seems to be burning up right in front of your eyes — this verse literally says *you will be saved yet so as by fire.* This means when the fire is done and gone what you've built wrongly will be consumed and devoured. In fact, when verse 15 says, "yet so as by fire," it means *he will survive with the smell of smoke on his clothes.* While this might seem tragic, it is actually good news! The fire may burn everything on top of the foundation, but your foundation will *always* remain — *you can't burn up Jesus!*

If Jesus is your foundation, then no matter what you've built on top, you will always have a sturdy foundation beneath your life. And once you've discovered the things in your life that you have built poorly, you are perfectly positioned to start again! All because you chose your foundation wisely and even after a fire it is still in place.

The following is a personal testimony from Rick Renner that illustrates why building your foundation upon Jesus Christ is so important:

> Nearly 30 years ago when Denise and I first moved to the former Soviet Union, we were about to open our first office in Moscow, Russia. We were still living in Riga, Latvia at the time, and I was going back and forth to Moscow almost every week, so I was kind of in a rush to get our office open. I *really* wanted to be able to say we had an office in Moscow, and rather than do things correctly and take my time, I did things very fast. Oftentimes when you do things too fast, you do things wrong.

> I even heard the Holy Spirit say to me, "Slow down. You need to slow down and really check out what you're doing. Make sure you're building this office correctly." But I was in a rush — I had my mind set on having that office in Moscow.

And guess what? We had an office in Moscow, but it didn't last
very long. A little fire came — it wasn't even a big fire, just a little
one — and it blew everything to smithereens because I built it
incorrectly.

But the foundation of Jesus was still in place. Even though
we figuratively had the smell of smoke on our clothes, we just
brushed it off and said, "Hey, let's do this again. And this time
we're going to learn from that bad lesson and open a new office
that will be built correctly." So that's precisely what we did.

This was such a critical lesson in my life. It taught me that *it's better to move slowly and surely than to move fast and to build wrongly.*

That is the lesson found within First Corinthians 3:11-15. And, again,
verse 11 tells us, "For other foundation can no man lay than that is laid,
which is Jesus Christ." Jesus is your rock-solid foundation. He is under
you and will hold you and anything you choose to build on top of that
foundation up.

Quality Over Quantity

In verse 12, Paul asked about the *quality* of how people were choosing to
build their lives. It reads, "Now if any man builds upon this foundation
gold, silver, precious stones, wood, hay, stubble." From this we know that
God has given us responsibility and will hold us accountable for what we
use to construct our lives. And once again, we see a picture of buildings
made of materials that were built to last.

The reason Rome is such an amazing city is because those who built it
really had eternity in mind. They built buildings that are *still standing
in Rome to this day — that is amazing!* For example, if you go to the
Pantheon, it has been standing in the heart of Rome for *1800* years,
completely unfazed. You might be wondering, *How is it still standing?*
The people who built it were thinking long-term. They weren't in a hurry,
and they said, "We're going to build this building in a way that it will
last for ages and ages." And the Pantheon isn't just standing; it is still in
use today! This is all because of the mindset the builders had when it was
constructed.

But 2000 years ago, the Pantheon was surrounded by buildings that were
made of wood, hay, and stubble, and not one of those buildings is still

around today. Not even a fragment of them is left because those little shanties could not withstand the fire and went up in a fiery puff of smoke. The people who constructed their homes out of wood, hay, and stubble were not long-term thinkers.

In verse 13, Paul said, "Every man's work shall be made manifest…." This is a promise. It doesn't matter who you are or what you are building, *it is going to be made manifest*. And the verse goes on to say, "…For the day shall declare it, because it shall be revealed by fire…." In other words, the day will come when what you have built will be tested by fire and how you have built your life will be revealed.

But again, God is not sending the fire. God never sends anything destructive into your life. The enemy may send it, it may be a fire that is generated because of the world we live in, or it may even be a fire you've ignited because of some foolish thing you did. There are all kinds of reasons for destructive fires, but they're *never* from the Lord. And when they do come, they reveal what you've been building. The Bible even says you will be rewarded if your work abides and survives the fire (1 Corinthians 3:14). But remember, you will not be rewarded for the *quantity* of what you build; you will be rewarded for the *quality*.

Build a Life That Abides

Let's take another look at verse 14. It reads, "If any man's work abide…." The word "abide" is the Greek word *meno*, and it means *to stay, dwell, lodge, or continue*. This depicts a life that remains, stays put, and continues to dwell on the foundation it's been built on. So, again, this tells us that if any man's work survives and passes the test of fire, he will receive a reward.

So how do you build a life that abides? As we have learned, a life that will last prioritizes quality over quantity, and that means building things with long-term thinking. For example, look at your finances. Are you spending your money as it comes in, or do you have a long-term plan? Are you really planning for your future? A day will come when a fire blows in, and it will reveal whether what you're doing with your finances will last through the flames or not.

Or how about your children? Are you spending quality time with each of your children and giving them what they need, or are you letting the television be your babysitter? A day will come when what you've been putting into your children will be revealed. Or what about your marriage? Are you spending time with your spouse and investing in one another? Are you treating that relationship like it's the most important relationship in your life? A day will come when your kids move out and it's just you and your spouse. That day will reveal what you have built into your marriage, and unfortunately, many people find out that they didn't invest enough in their marriage.

From this lesson, you have learned that a day will eventually come that will test what you have built in your life. And if a fire comes, and you realize, *Wow — what I built is standing and has survived every test*, you have something to rejoice about! But even if the fire comes and burns everything up, you still have something to rejoice about because the foundation of Jesus Christ is underneath you and can never be destroyed.

Because of the rock-solid foundation of Jesus Christ, you can say, "You know what, I've made some mistakes in the past, but I'm not going to make them again. Because Jesus is under me, I can start over and begin to do things wisely this time, with long-term thinking, and build my life and everything in it with quality." *That* is what you're going to be rewarded for!

STUDY QUESTIONS

Study to shew thyself approved unto God, a workman that needeth not to be ashamed, rightly dividing the word of truth.
— 2 Timothy 2:15

1. Why do things built with wood, hay, and stubble not last? How does having Jesus as your foundation help you if you discover you've been building your life with vulnerable and feeble materials?
2. What does it mean to build your foundation on Jesus?
3. What does it mean to have your work "revealed by fire"?

PRACTICAL APPLICATION

But be doers of the word, and not hearers only,
deceiving your own selves.
—James 1:22

1. Take a moment to think about the areas in your life where you may have built too quickly or hastily. What happened? What can you do differently next time you build in those areas?

2. Take a moment to assess how you're building your life *right now*. Ask yourself if you're building for *quantity* or *quality*. If you're not building for quality, what are some changes you can make in your life today to make sure what you are building will last?

TOPIC

It's Time for You To Start Using the Gifts and Talents God Gave You

Editor's Note: This lesson was taken from Rick Renner's *Sparkling Gems From the Greek, Volume 2:* September 30. *Sparkling Gems From the Greek* is a daily devotional from the Greek language of the New Testament.

SCRIPTURES

1. **1 Peter 4:9** — Use hospitality one to another without grudging.

2. **1 Peter 4:10** — As every man hath received the gift, even so minister the same one to another, as good stewards of the manifold grace of God.

3. **1 Peter 4:11** — If any man speak, let him speak as the oracles of God; if any man minister, let him do it as of the ability which God giveth: that God in all things may be glorified through Jesus Christ, to whom be praise and dominion for ever and ever. Amen.

4. **1 Peter 4:11** (*RIV*) — Every single one of you without exception has received a grace-given gift from God. Embrace what God has placed inside you. Take ownership of it, and do your best to use that special gift to meet the needs of one another. God has entrusted a lot to you by placing those special gifts in your life, and he's depending on you to be faithful with this great responsibility.

GREEK WORDS

1. "every man" — ἕκαστος (*hekastos*): an all-inclusive term that embraces everyone, with no one excluded

2. "received" — **λαμβάνω** (*lambano*): to receive or to take; to take hold of something to make it one's own

3. "gift" — **χάρις** (*charis*): the word for grace; used here to refer to grace-given gifts

4. "minister" — **διακονέω** (*diakoneo*): a high-level servant; pictured serving in a way that was honorable, pleasurable, and done in a fashion that made the people being served feel as if they were nobility

5. "minister the same one to another" — **ἑαυτοῦ** (*heautou*): reciprocal ministry

6. "steward" — **οἰκονόμος** (*oikonomos*): a person who is put in charge of another person's household; a household administrator

7. "ability" — **ἰσχύς** (*ischus*): a man covered in muscles; a strong man or a mighty man

SYNOPSIS

If you have been born again, according to First Peter 4:10 God has graced you with a unique and special gift. But in order to operate in this gift, you must receive it, cultivate it, and faithfully serve those around you with it. You can't just expect to be naturally good at your gift — you have to take ownership of it and put in the work to truly excel and utilize it so God's manifold grace will shine through you and minister to others.

The emphasis of the lesson:

Every believer without exception has received a grace-given gift from God. As you identify, embrace, cultivate, and use your gifts, God will empower you with the strength and wisdom you need to master them and serve at the highest level possible. But what is the goal or objective of this? In this lesson, you will discover that taking ownership of your gifts and ministering to others with them will cause people to take notice of the grace of God that is operating and shining through you. The objective is for God to be glorified in *all things*, including our gifts!

In this program, Rick shared a little secret habit that he does before every TV program he films and before every sermon he preaches. It comes from First Peter 4:9, which says, "Use hospitality one to another without grudging." Rick always reads this verse before he sits down to minister to you on his daily programs because it says to "use hospitality." Reading this verse reminds him to throw open the door and warmly welcome his viewers to the program and to do so without grudging.

It doesn't matter what's going on in his life or how tired he is, when Rick sits down in his chair in the TV studio and begins talking to you, he always wants you to feel welcomed. Putting this verse at the front of his mind helps Rick ensure he is using hospitality. In this lesson, you will learn about the grace-given gifts God has placed inside you and how you are to be accountable and responsible for the way you utilize them.

Every Believer Is Gifted, Including You!

In First Peter 4:10, the Bible tells us:

As every man hath received the gift, even so minister the same one to another, as good stewards of the manifold grace of God.

Look at the very beginning of verse 10. Peter said, "As every man hath received the gift…." In Greek, the words "every man" are the word *hekastos*, and it means *every single person without exception.* In the context of this verse, it means every believer in the Body of Christ, including you, has received a gift. That is *explicitly* what this verse means.

You need to quit saying, "Oh, I wish I was gifted like other people," because *you are gifted!* Every single person without exception has received a gift from God. The word "received" is the Greek word *lambano*, which means *to receive,* but it also means *to take.* This tells us that while God definitely gives gifts to each of us, *we also have to take them.*

We must take ownership of our God-given gifts and choose to receive them. Ask yourself, "Have I really received what God has given to me? Have I embraced His gifts in my life?"

In fact, the word "received" doesn't just mean to receive or take, but it also carries the idea of *cultivation.* You have to take hold of your gift and say, "God, I'm going to develop the gift you've given me." The word "gift" used in First Peter 4:10 is a form of the Greek word *charis,* and it is the word for *grace.* These are *grace-given gifts.* They aren't something you're naturally born with. These are gifts that have been supernaturally imparted to you by God.

For example, Rick's ability to teach the Bible is a grace-given gift, and he had to receive it. Not only did he have to receive it, but God expected him to do something with it. He had to take ownership of his gift, cultivate it, and develop it in order to excel in it.

When you wrap your arms around the *charis*, or grace-given gift, God has given you, suddenly you are empowered to do what you could never do by yourself. You are gifted to do what you would never have done on your own because it is a grace-given.

You might be thinking, *This is great, but how do I know what my grace-given gift is?* Start by praying in tongues and searching the scriptures to discover what your gift is. And you definitely have one because First Peter 4:10 says "every man," or *hekastos*, has a gift, meaning every single believer without exception has received a God-given gift, including you!

You Are Called to High-Level Service

Let's take another look at First Peter 4:10. It reads:

As every man hath received the gift, even so minister the same one to another, as good stewards of the manifold grace of God.

What does the phrase "even so minister" mean? The word "minister" is a form of the Greek word *diakoneo*, and it is the same word translated as "deacons" in Acts 6:1 and 2. But the word *diakoneo* used in this verse is the word "minister," which was a word used to describe *high-level servants*. These servants served tables in very luxurious, wealthy homes. They had to learn how to serve and how to speak correctly and politely to the people they were serving who came from diverse cultural backgrounds. These servants were excellently trained and mastered the skill of serving.

There is a restaurant in Moscow that Rick and Denise love to go to called The House of Writers. It's a very old restaurant, and it's pretty amazing. When they serve you in this restaurant, the waiters are dressed in tuxedos with bowties, and when they bring your food to the table, every dish is not only beautifully displayed on the plate, but the way they bring the food to the table itself is an experience. The servers at this restaurant make you feel like royalty, and that is what the word "minister" in First Peter 4:10 describes.

The word "minister" tells us that we not only need to take the gift God has given us and cultivate or take ownership of it, but we also need to become *the best* we can at ministering and serving with whichever grace-given gift has been bestowed upon us. For example, it isn't enough for Rick to sit in his chair and film a program without any preparation. That would result in a sloppily delivered message. Instead, God expects him to bring the *highest level* of service to you, and that's why he spends many, many hours preparing every single program and lesson.

It doesn't matter what your gift is, whether it's singing, serving, teaching, preaching, or working in the children's ministry. If your gift is to be an usher at church, God expects you to be the very best usher you can be. *Whatever* you're doing, God wants you to provide the highest level of service possible!

Ask yourself, "What kind of service am I rendering with the gift God has given me? Is it high-level service?" This is what First Peter 4:10 says God expects of us.

Verse 10 also says, "…Even so minister the same one to another.…" The phrase "the same one to another" is translated as the Greek word *heautou*, and it describes *reciprocal ministry*. We are not only expected to minister with our gifts, but we are also expected to receive ministry from others. The Body of Christ is to be a place where there is reciprocal ministry as each person uses their God-given gifts.

The verse goes on to say:

> **…Even so minister the same one to another, as good stewards of the manifold grace of God.**
>
> **— 1 Peter 4:10**

The word "steward" is the Greek word *oikonomos*, which describes *a person who was put in charge of another person's household.* This trusted person would have been responsible for paying the bills, paying the employees, and the overall condition of the house. Even though the house was not his own, he was put in charge of the household and the owner held him responsible for all the affairs of the house. The use of this word in verse 10 tells us that God really expects us to take ownership of the gifts He has given us, and He's going to hold us accountable for what we do with the grace-given gifts that have been imparted to us.

You Were Made To Shine Differently!

Notice First Peter 4:10 says, "…Good stewards of the *manifold* grace of God." The word "manifold" can be translated as *variegated* or *multifaceted*, and it is the exact word used in the Old Testament Septuagint to describe

Joseph's coat of many colors. The use of this word in verse 10 tells us God's gifts are variegated and multifaceted.

There was a time earlier in Rick's life when he really put himself down because he wasn't like others. Rick and Denise would go to ministers' conferences, and the whole time they sat and listened to the other pastors preach, rather than enjoy their teaching, Rick would be putting himself down. He would say to himself, "I can't shout like that. I can't scream like that. I can't preach like he can. I can't run in the auditorium like that; it's just not who I am." He really put himself down because he thought he couldn't fit in or be like everybody else.

One day while Rick was sitting in a meeting, comparing himself to others and putting himself down, the Holy Spirit spoke to him and said, "I made you shine *differently* than others." At that moment something inside him woke up, and he realized, *You know what, they can't do what I do!* It suddenly occurred to him that while he was teaching, other people could have the same exact thoughts Rick was having while he compared himself to them.

That is why the Bible explicitly says we're not wise when we compare ourselves among ourselves (*see* 2 Corinthians 10:12). We are not to compare ourselves to others because the gifts and grace of God are *multifaceted*.

It's like when you hold a diamond up to the light, and it begins to refract a prism of beautiful colors and shades. Those different colors and shades are like the gifts of God, and rather than put yourself down because your gift is different than someone else's, you need to say, "You know what, this is the gift God gave me! I'm going to embrace it and be a good steward of it. God is going to hold me accountable for it, so I'm going to take ownership of my gift and develop it in order to give the highest level of service I can with what God has given to me." If you make that kind of commitment in your heart, you will begin to sparkle and shine, and those around will love receiving from your particular and unique gift.

Everyone has a niche of their own. You don't have to be like somebody else — *God has made you shine a little differently than everyone else* because you have received a gift from the multifaceted, manifold grace of God!

Using Your Gifts Glorifies God

So, as we have learned, First Peter 4:10 says:

**As every man hath received the gift, even so minister the same
one to another, as good stewards of the manifold grace of God.**

And verse 11 goes on to tell us:

**If any man speak, let him speak as the oracles of God; if any
man minister, let him do it as of the ability which God giveth….**

Here we have the word "minister" again. It is the Greek word *diakoneo*,
which means *high-level service*. In everything you do, are you really giving
your best to Jesus? Are you showing up late to serve God's people, or are
you on time? Do you look like you are prepared to serve, or do you look
like you got ready in the car on the way to the meeting? Did you really
take the time to pray and to develop and prepare your gift before you
arrived? These are all things you should be asking yourself in order to
provide *diakoneo*, the highest level of service possible.

We need to give our *very, very* best to whatever grace-given gift has been
placed in our lives. Notice verse 11 says, "…If any man minister, let him
do it as of the ability which God giveth…." The word "ability" is a form of
the Greek word *ischus*, which describes *a man who is covered with muscles.*
It depicts a man who is muscle-bound, or a mighty, mighty muscular man.

In the context of First Peter 4:11, you will find that when you take ownership of your grace-given gift from God and do your best to prepare and
begin to operate in it, *God will release all His mighty power to flow through
you!* That is what grace does — *it empowers you.* It's God's mighty power,
flowing through you to be more and do more than you ever could by
yourself. God's power flows through your grace-given gift and empowers
you to operate in it!

The Bible even tells us why God empowers these grace-given gifts in our
lives. First Peter 4:11 continues, saying:

**…That God in all things may be glorified through Jesus Christ,
to whom be praise and dominion for ever and ever. Amen.**

That is the objective. We have not been given gifts so that people will
appreciate and admire the way we are shining. We have been given these
gifts so that people will say, "Amazing! That is such a gift from God!" The
objective is to diligently serve with our gifts in such a way that people
stand in amazement at God shining through you because when you use
your gifts well, it brings glory to God!

For example, someone might be gifted to conduct interviews on television. Not everyone can do that, but some people can conduct interviews *masterfully*. This person isn't just naturally good at TV interviews; God has given them the strength and skill to do the job really well.

Another example is when Rick stands at the pulpit or comes on television to bring you the teaching of the Bible. He doesn't want you to be impressed with him and his own abilities. He wants you to say, "*Wow, what a gift of God in action!*" Your gift is not about you or anybody else — *it's about God and that in all things He may be glorified!*

We bring glory to God when we diligently and faithfully cultivate and use our grace-given gifts. And all of this is found in First Peter 4:11. With this in mind, the *Renner Interpretive Version* of First Peter 4:11 reads:

> **Every single one of you without exception has received a grace-given gift from God. Embrace what God has placed inside you. Take ownership of it, and do your best to use that special gift to meet the needs of one another. God has entrusted a lot to you by placing those special gifts in your life, and He is depending on you to be faithful with this great responsibility.**

That is amazing! When you embrace the gift God has placed inside you and take ownership of it, it brings glory to God. Not only that, but God is also expecting you to use that special gift to faithfully minister to the needs of other people. Let's take another look at the verse Rick reads before filming TV programs or speaking publicly. It says:

> **Use hospitality one to another without grudging.**
>
> **— 1 Peter 4:9**

If you're tempted to say, "I'm just not good enough for this," then you're grudging. Or if you're tempted to say, "I don't want to be here," you're grudging. You have to say *no* to that kind of attitude. Instead, you need to speak confidence and encouragement to yourself and say, "*This is my moment to shine!* This is the moment when my gift is needed. I'm saying *no* to me, and I'm putting aside whatever is going on in my life. From the moment I open my mouth or begin to serve, I'm going to use hospitality to roll out the red carpet and welcome every single person with outstretched arms and the highest level of service possible." That is what God is expecting of you.

God wants you to shine with the manifold grace of God. He's given you
a gift — and you may not know what that gift is yet, but if you will pray
in tongues, spend time in the Word, and serve, you will discover your gift.
When you discover it, you need to take ownership of it, develop it, and
begin serving the very best you can. And God will empower you with the
strength you need to do it!

STUDY QUESTIONS

> **Study to shew thyself approved unto God, a workman that
> needeth not o be ashamed, rightly dividing the word of truth.**
> **— 2 Timothy 2:15**

1. Have you identified any grace-given gifts that God has placed in your
   life? If so, what steps have you taken to develop and cultivate these
   gifts so that God's grace can shine through your life to others?

2. How can you discover what gift God has graced you with?

3. In this lesson, you saw that the word "minister" is the Greek word
   diakoneo, which means *high-level service*. What is high-level service,
   and what does it have to do with ministering in your grace-given gift?

PRACTICAL APPLICATION

> **But be ye doers of the word, and not hearers only,**
> **deceiving your own selves.**
> **— James 1:22**

1. Have you noticed any results from allowing the gifts God has given
   you to shine through you?

2. First Peter 4:10 says, "…Every man hath received the gift, even so
   minister the same one to another, as good stewards of the manifold
   grace of God." In other words, every single born-again believer has
   been given a special gift from God. Reflect on your grace-given gifts
   and make a list of ways you believe God wants His grace to flow
   through your life to reach others.

3. Have you ever felt like you're not good enough to operate in your
   grace-given gift because you're different? Or have you focused your
   time on comparing yourself with others and their gifts? According
   to the Bible, the gifts of God are multifaceted, and He made you

to shine differently than others. How does this encourage you to embrace and take ownership of the gifts God has placed in your life?

TOPIC

Perilous Times Shall Come

Editor's Note: This lesson was taken from Rick Renner's *Sparkling Gems From the Greek, Volume 2:* May 10 and May 11. *Sparkling Gems From the Greek* is a daily devotional from the Greek language of the New Testament.

SCRIPTURES

1. **2 Timothy 3:1** — This know also, that in the last days perilous times shall come.

2. **Matthew 8:28** — And when he was come to the other side into the country of the Gergesenes, there met him two possessed with devils, coming out of the tombs, exceeding fierce, so that no man might pass by that way.

3. **2 Peter 3:1** — This second epistle, beloved, I now wrote unto you; in both which I stir up your pure minds by way of remembrance.

4. **2 Peter 3:9** — The Lord is not slack concerning his promise, as some men count slackness; but is longsuffering to us-ward, not willing that any should perish, but that all should come to repentance.

GREEK WORDS

1. "know" — γίνωσκε (*ginoske*): a direct form of the word γινώσκω (*ginosko*), meaning I know; used to draw attention to a message so critical that it must be known, recognized, and acknowledged

2. "that" — ὅτι (*hoti*): a pointer word used to draw attention to what comes after it

3. "last" — ἐσχάταις (*eschatais*): a form of the word ἔσχατος (*eschatos*), meaning the very last or ultimate end of something

4. "perilous" — χαλεπός (*chalepos*): dangerous, risky, or harmful; pictures something that is wounding or injurious

5. "shall come" — ἐνίστημι (*enistemi*): a compound of the word ἐν (*en*), which means to be in, and the word ἵστημι (*histemi*), which means to stand; compounded together it describes an environment standing all around you or what encumbers you and surrounds you; to be surrounded on every side so that you don't see how you can get through

6. "slack" — βραδύνω (*braduno*): tardy, slow, delayed, or late in time

SYNOPSIS

According to the Bible, the last days will be a time of delusional thinking, chaos, and moral corruption. Indeed, perilous times will come, and in this lesson, you will discover exactly what these "perilous times" entail. You will also discover the indicators believers can look for that signify the very end of the last days as well as the crucial assignment God has handed to His Church and why the Lord has delayed His second coming.

The emphasis of this lesson:

The apostle Paul gave a warning to believers in Second Timothy 3:1 when he wrote, "This know also, that in the last days perilous times shall come." This warning was not designed to scare us but to prepare us. We aren't called to flee or hide — we are called to exercise the authority of Jesus, stand firm in our faith, and remember that God has called us to win souls. That is to be our focus, even in perilous times.

As a born-again believer, you have probably heard teaching on the end times or the last days, but what does the Bible tell us about the last days? In Second Timothy 3, the Holy Spirit spoke through the apostle Paul in order to alert and prepare believers around the world for the perilous times ahead.

The Days We Are Living In

In Second Timothy 3, Paul wrote about the last days as he was led by the Holy Spirit to write. It was like the Holy Spirit pointed His prophetic finger into the future and described to Paul precisely what the world would be like at the end of the present age.

The entire chapter of Second Timothy 3 really describes the times we are living in today, but verse 1 is foundational to this chapter. It reads:

This know also, that in the last days perilous times shall come.
— 2 Timothy 3:1

To fully understand what Paul was writing about in this verse, we must look at it piece by piece, starting with the word "know." The word "know" is the Greek word *ginoske*, which is a form of the word *ginosko* meaning *I know*. But the word *ginoske* in Second Timothy 3:1 is a very direct form of this word. It was as if Paul lifted his voice, saying, "Pay attention! *This is something that must be known!*"

Paul then went on to describe what will happen at the end of the age. And he didn't write these things to scare us. The Holy Spirit moved on Paul to write these things in order to *prepare* us. God loves us so much that He wants everyone, especially those who are living in the end times, to know what is coming so we will be well prepared for it. That is why the tone of Paul's language is so strong in this verse.

The next word to notice in Second Timothy 3:1 is "that," which is the Greek word *hoti*. *Hoti* is what Rick often refers to as *a pointer word*, and through it the Holy Spirit is pointing at exactly what you must know, acknowledge, embrace, and understand: "…That in the last days, *perilous times shall come.*"

Some people might be tempted to say, "Christians have been calling this the 'last days' for 2,000 years." But guess what? They are actually right because the last 2,000 years are what the Bible describes as the last days. In Acts 2, Peter prophesied that in the last days God would pour out His Spirit upon all flesh (*see* Acts 2:17), and that is exactly what happened on the day of Pentecost. It triggered the beginning of the period that we know today as *the last days*.

Some people also call this time period the Age of Grace or the Church Age, but all of these terms describe the last days which began on the day of Pentecost. That means every event that took place after the day of Pentecost in the New Testament actually happened at the beginning of the end times.

When you come to Second Timothy 3:1, the Holy Spirit is pointing His finger into the future, all the way to the very last of the last days. He's not pointing to the beginning of that 2,000-year period, but *all the way to the very, very end*. In fact, the word "last" is the Greek word *eschatos*, and it's where we get the term for eschatology, which describes end time events or the study of the last days. And the word *eschatos* is really important to this verse because it describes *the very ultimate end of a thing*.

For example, the word *eschatos* could describe the last day of the week. It could also describe the last day of the month or the last day of the year, but it *only* describes *the very last day*. It can be used in a navigational sense to describe the very farthest end of the earth. For instance, you could use *eschatos* to indicate you had gone somewhere and there was nowhere else to go because you'd gone all the way to the end. The word *eschatos* could also be used to describe a ship that has sailed to its final port. It would communicate that the ship's journey was over because it had reached its final destination. That is what the word *eschatos* means.

It's remarkable that the Holy Spirit accurately forecasted what would happen at the very end of the age. He pointed to the final wrap up of the last days in Second Timothy 3:1, and this verse really is talking about the days we're currently living in. Through the words of Paul, the Holy Spirit is urging each of us to emphatically know, to acknowledge, and to understand that in our current age, in the last of the last days, *perilous times shall come*.

'Perilous Times' — A Sign of the End of the Age

The word "perilous" in Second Timothy 3:1 is the Greek word *chalepos*, which describes *something that is hurtful, harmful, dangerous, and injurious*. If you were to get too close to something that was perilous, you would need to be careful because it would be filled with danger — it would be filled with risk, harm, and peril. That is what the word "perilous" means. And it is only used in one other place in the *entire* New Testament.

To better understand this word, let's take a look at its second use in Matthew 8:28. It says:

> **And when he was come to the other side into the country of the Gergesenes, there met him two possessed with devils, coming out of the tombs, exceeding fierce, so that no man might pass by that way.**

This verse is often a point of contention for people because they think there's a mistake. Mark 5 says there was only one demon possessed man, but Matthew says there were two. Some people think these two gospel writers got their facts messed up, but in reality, there *were* two possessed men. The author of the book of Mark always dealt with the more serious instances of Jesus' ministry, so he only described the worse of the two demon possessed men.

Matthew 8:28 tells us both of these demon possessed men lived in the tombs. If you were ever to visit this place in Israel, you would see many cliffs and an old cemetery very close to the sea. You would also see a road which leads from the north to the south of the sea. For the people who lived on that side of the Sea of Galilee, taking this road south was the quickest way for them to get to the city of Jerusalem, and the Bible says these demon possessed men lived in the tombs near this road.

According to Matthew 8:28, these men were "exceedingly fierce," which is the Greek word *chalepos* — the same word translated as "perilous" in Second Timothy 3:1. This means that these men were *so treacherous* they posed risk, harm, and hurt to anyone who came through that area. When people tried to take that road near the sea, the possessed men would charge out of the tombs. The men were so completely demonized that they would terrorize everyone who traveled along that road. People became afraid to take that road, and as a result, these men became *an impasse.*

This has a lot to do with what we're studying in Second Timothy 3:1, which says, "...Perilous times shall come." The word "perilous" implies the last days are going to become so risky, so dangerous, and so harmful that society at large as well as the Church will say, "We've hit an impasse. How are we ever going to get through what we're dealing with?"

In fact, if you look at the world around you, you will see people are being damaged at every level. They're altering the way they think, and they are leaving the truth of the Word of God behind. They're making wrong moral choices, which is so dangerous. And people are defiling themselves in the way they think and in their relationships. We're living in the day of reprobate minds — we really are.

If you take a look around, you will see you are surrounded by nonsense, delusional thinking, and peril. *Welcome to the last days!* And there's something else, Second Timothy 3:1 says, "...Perilous times shall come." The word "times" is a Greek word that describes *decades,* as in one decade coming after another. These perilous times may begin slowly, but they will begin snowballing until, finally, they will begin to move at the speed of light.

And things are changing so fast, it's shocking. For example, news articles have been written that some state and world powers are attempting to put to a vote that adults can legally have sex with minors if those minors, even children, are consenting to it! *What are we doing!*

We are not thinking right because we're living at the very end of the age when delusional thinking is going to rule society. These are the times we are living in, and if we believe what the Bible says, it's only going to get even crazier as we get closer to the very end of days.

This is really what Paul wrote in Second Timothy 3:1. He essentially said, "If you begin to see this kind of wrong and delusional thinking become more prominent, that is a sign you are at the very end of the age. You have sailed to the last port, and there's not much time left for your journey."

Perilous Times 'Shall Come'

But there's something else we need to pay attention to in this verse:

This know also, that in the last days perilous time shall come.
— 2 Timothy 3:1

Notice the words "shall come," which are the Greek word *enistemi*. *Enistemi* is a compound of the word *en*, which means *to be in*, and the word *histemi*, meaning *to stand*. When you put these two words together, it describes *an environment standing all around you* or *what surrounds you*. In other words, the Holy Spirit is saying through this verse if you've come to a point where you are surrounded on every side and you don't see how you can get through, it's an impasse. And if everywhere you look you see crazy and delusional thinking and wrong moral decisions, you have come to the very end of the age because these are signs that indicate you're living in the last of days.

It's also interesting that Paul wrote in Second Peter 3 another sign you are living in the last of days is people will sneer and mock those who believe they're living in the last days. They will say, "What is this business about the rapture of the Church and the end of the age? People have been saying that since the beginning of Creation!" The Bible says that when people begin to wag their tongues and make fun of the rapture and the coming of the Lord, questioning its validity, it's yet another sign that you've come to the end of the age.

The Second Coming of Jesus

But why doesn't the Lord come back sooner? Why is He delaying His coming? Let's take a look at Second Peter 3 to find out. It says:

> **The Lord is not slack concerning his promise, as some men count slackness....**
>
> —2 Peter 3:9

The word "promise" refers to the promise of the Lord's coming, and the word "slack" is the Greek word *braduno*, which describes something that is *tardy, slow,* or *late.* In other words, the Lord is not a minute late concerning the promise of His coming. So what is stopping Him from coming? The Bible says:

> **...[The Lord is] not willing that any should perish....**
>
> —2 Peter 3:9

The words "not willing" don't mean that people aren't going to perish, but they do indicate that if God really had His way, He wouldn't want *anyone* to perish. He has put the whole thing on pause and is waiting for the last person to repent. That is also why the end of this verse says, "...But that all should come to repentance."

That is the heart of God. Rather than worry and fret over what you're going to do, you need to understand that this is your moment to rescue the perishing and care for the dying. Jesus is coming, but He hasn't come yet because He's waiting for the last person to be saved. And when that last person is saved, the rapture of the Church is going to take place. *Wouldn't it be wonderful if you were the one who led that last person to Christ?*

God wants to use you to reach out to those that are living in harm's way. And rather than hide, we need to do what Jesus did in Matthew 8:28 when He saw the demonized men. Jesus didn't jump back into His boat and flee. That situation beckoned Him to action, so Jesus got out of the boat and moved toward that impasse. He moved toward that peril and exercised His authority to change the situation.

We have the Word of God, the power of the Holy Spirit, the blood of Jesus, and everything we need to step forward into darkness in order to rescue the perishing, care for the dying, and help those who are in harm's way. That is God's assignment to us in these last days — that even though perilous times shall come, we have the amazing opportunity to prepare and save as many people as we can before Jesus comes again.

STUDY QUESTIONS

Study to shew thyself approved unto God, a workman that needeth not to be ashamed, rightly dividing the word of truth.
— 2 Timothy 2:15

1. According to Second Peter 3:9, *why* has the Lord delayed His second coming? What is He waiting for?

2. What are the signs that Christians can use to recognize we are living in the very last of days?

3. In this lesson, you saw that the word "perilous" from Second Timothy 3:1 is the Greek word *chalepos*, and this word only appears in one other place in the New Testament. What does the use of this word in Matthew 8:28 tell us about the end of the age?

PRACTICAL APPLICATION

But be ye doers of the word, and not hearers only,
deceiving your own selves.
— James 1:22

1. Are you tempted to be in fear about the perilous times ahead? What are some ways you can exercise the authority of Jesus during these times? Take a moment to list them.

2. There are many people today who are in denial and doubt about living in the last days. They are blinded by delusional thinking, and they are in harm's way. Pause for a moment to pray for these people. Pray their eyes would be opened and they would wake up to the severity of their situation so that they may be born again.

TOPIC

Equipped To Sail Victorious Through Stormy Times

Editor's Note: This lesson was taken from Rick Renner's *Sparkling Gems From the Greek, Volume 2:* September 22 and 23. *Sparkling Gems From the Greek* is a daily devotional from the Greek language of the New Testament.

SCRIPTURES

1. **2 Timothy 3:1** — This know also, that in the last days perilous times shall come.

2. **2 Timothy 3:13** — But evil men and seducers shall wax worse and worse, deceiving, and being deceived.

3. **2 Timothy 3:14** — But continue thou in the things which thou hast learned and hast been assured of, knowing of whom thou hast learned them.

4. **2 Timothy 3:16,17** — All scripture is given by inspiration of God, and is profitable for doctrine, for reproof, for correction, for instruction in righteousness: that the man of God may be perfect, thoroughly furnished unto all good works.

GREEK WORDS

1. "know" — γίνωσκε (*ginoske*): a direct form of the word γινώσκω (*ginosko*), meaning I know; used to draw attention to a message so critical that it must be known, recognized, and acknowledged

2. "that" — ὅτι (*hoti*): a pointer word used to draw attention to what comes after it

3. "last" — ἐσχάταις (*eschatais*): a form of the word ἔσχατος (*eschatos*), meaning the very last or ultimate end of something

4. "perilous" — χαλεπός (*chalepos*): dangerous, risky, or harmful; pictures something that is wounding or injurious

5. "shall come" — ἐνίστημι (*enistemi*): a compound of the word ἐν (*en*), which means to be in, and the word ἵστημι (*histemi*), which means to stand; compounded together it describes an environment standing all around you or what encumbers you and surrounds you; to be surrounded on every side so that you don't see how you can get through

6. "continue" — μένω (*meno*): to stay, remain, or abide; to firmly endure; used to describe soldiers who were charged to watch over a piece of land that had been entrusted into their care

7. "inspiration of God" — θεόπνευστος (*theopneustos*): from θεός (*theos*) the word for God and πνέω (*pneo*), which describes a dynamic movement of air; compounded together it means God breathed the Scriptures out and released creative power, produced a new sound of music, and imparted a new fragrance

8. "inspiration" — πνέω (*pneo*): the Old Testament word for creative power; the word for air that is blown from the mouth into a wind instrument to produce music; the ancient word for perfume

9. "man of God" — ἄνθρωπος (*anthropos*): a man or human; refers to anyone belonging to God

10. "perfect" — ἄρτιος (*artios*): mature; fitted or complete; completely sufficient in every way

SYNOPSIS

As a believer, it can sometimes be challenging to not worry about the last days, especially knowing that according to Second Timothy 3:1, "…in the last days perilous times shall come." But you don't have to worry because God has already supplied you with everything you need to weather the storm. His inspired Word contains the power to transform your life and equip you to face every challenge with the confidence that He will carry you through to the other side.

The emphasis of this lesson:

We are living in the very last of the last days, and you need to be prepared for what is coming. That is why the Word of God is vital to every believer. It is not only God-breathed and inspired — but God Himself is within every word and page. Once you realize the divine power His Word contains and begin to spend time in it, you will release the very DNA of God into your life and become a partaker of all He has to offer!

The Word of God is truly the only way to be thoroughly equipped to sail victoriously through these stormy times.

The Very End of the Last Days

This know also, that in the last days perilous times shall come.
— 2 Timothy 3:1

As we learned in the previous lesson, the word "know" is the Greek word *ginoske*, a form of the word *ginosko*, meaning *I know*. But as the direct form *ginoske*, it means *you must know this, you must understand this*, and *you must acknowledge this*. In Second Timothy 3:1, the Holy Spirit is telling those who are living at the end of the age — those of us living today — that there is something vital for them to know and understand.

But remember, the Holy Spirit isn't telling us these things to scare us; He wants to prepare us. The verse goes on to say, "This know also, *that*...." Here the Holy Spirit is referencing something very specific. The word "that" is the Greek word *hoti*, which is a pointer word. This means the Holy Spirit is saying that *specifically* in the last days, perilous times shall come.

We also saw the word "last" is the Greek word *eschatos*, which describes *the very ultimate end of a thing*. It was also used to describe the ends of the earth or a ship that has sailed to the very last port, signifying the end of the journey. And when the apostle Paul wrote "in the last days," he was not just describing the larger 2,000-year period called the last days. He was really referring to the very ultimate end of the last days. You could even translate the end of this verse as, "...when time has sailed to the last port and there is little time left in the journey perilous times shall come."

In our last lesson, we also learned the word "perilous" is the Greek word *chalepos*. It describes times that are filled with *peril, danger, risk*, and *harm*. Again, the reason the Holy Spirit is so explicit about what will happen during the last days is because these are the days we are living in today. He used specific language to draw our attention to what is ahead so that we can prepare ourselves in order to protect ourselves and our loved ones from harm. He does not want us to be subjected to the peril and danger that are indicative of the end times; He wants us to be prepared for it.

And the final part of Second Timothy 3:1 says, "...Perilous times shall come." The words "shall come" in Greek are the word *enistemi* — a compound of the word *en,* meaning *to be in,* and the word *histemi,* which means *to stand.* In other words, the Holy Spirit is saying if you look around you and feel like you are surrounded by nonsense, delusion, and treachery, that is your indication that you are living in perilous times. It's like He's saying, "Welcome to the very end of the age. These are the last of the last days."

Remember, the word "last" is the Greek word *eschatos,* which describes *a ship that has sailed to the very last port.* Keep this word in mind as we continue on in this lesson. It will be helpful in understanding what comes next.

Do Not Be Deceived, Stick to the Word!

What else does Second Timothy 3 say about the end times? Let's take a look at verse 13, which states:

> **But evil men and seducers shall wax worse and worse, deceiving, and being deceived.**

You may be thinking, *What in the world does "wax worse and worse" mean?* The phrase "wax worse and worse" is from a Greek word that describes the advancement of a disease like cancer or gangrene, and the use of this phrase tells us that evil is going to eat through society like cancer cells take over the body. Verse 13 even goes on to say that those who promote this toxic, evil thinking will be "deceiving, and being deceived," meaning these people are really going to believe the nonsense they are promoting.

But why would people believe such things? They will believe it because their minds have become reprobate, and when your mind is reprobate, you believe delusional things. That is why in verse 14 Paul gave believers instructions on what to do when the world around you is reprobate and delusional. It says:

> **But continue thou in the things which thou hast learned and hast been assured of, knowing of whom thou hast learned them.**
> — 2 Timothy 3:14

The word "continue" is a form of the Greek word *meno,* and it means *to abide* or *to stay in the same spot.* It's a resolute decision that you are not moving from your position. You don't care what pressure is exerted against you to try and change your position — you have resolved not to budge or flinch. *You have anchored yourself in what you believe.*

The word *meno* was also used to describe *soldiers who were charged to watch over a piece of land that had been entrusted into their care.* From this we find that God has entrusted the Word of God to us to watch over and care for. It doesn't matter what kind of pressures try to get you to conform or compromise with society. Your job is to continue, stay where you are, and stick with what you believe in order to watch over what has been entrusted to you.

It is better to obey the Bible and continue in the things you have learned and have been assured of than to follow the ways of an increasingly delusional society. And when those who have become lost in nonsensical thinking return to God, they will have someone to come back to. They will be able to lean on you for guidance because you are anchored in truth. It's not you that has changed, but the world around you. And to remain unaffected by society, you have to stick with what you believe.

In verse 14, Paul meant that we are to continue studying and abiding by the Word of God. We are living in a day when people are saying the Scriptures are bigoted or narrow-minded, and instead, they are looking to have a more progressive and open-minded way of thinking. It's always good to be open-minded, but don't be so open-minded that your brain falls out! Stick with the Word of God, and it will help you think clearly.

The Bible — The Life, Breath, and Power of God

Let's take a look at Second Timothy 3:16 and 17. It says:

All scripture is given by inspiration of God, and is profitable for doctrine, for reproof, for correction, for instruction in righteousness: that the man of God may be perfect, thoroughly furnished unto all good works.

Notice the beginning of verse 16 says, "All scripture is given by inspiration of God...." What does that mean? Poetry is a wonderful form of writing, but it is not divinely inspired. The Bible, on the other hand, is different. It's in a category all by itself because it was given "by *inspiration of God.*" This phrase is the Greek word *theopneustos*, which is a compound of the word *theos*, the word for *God*, and the word *pneustos*. The word *pneustos* comes from the root word *pneo*, which describes *a dynamic movement of air*, and in the form *pneustos*, it describes *a spirit, life*, or *divine energy.* When you combine these two words, *theopneustos* means *God-breathed* or *the Spirit of God breathed it out.*

That may sound confusing, but here is an illustration. If you took a balloon and blew on top of it, it would just be a balloon you are blowing on. But if you lifted that balloon to your lips and blew *into* the balloon, it would begin to expand. The more you breathed into it, the more it would expand until, finally, you tied a knot at the end to capture all your breath inside the balloon. And as a result, the balloon would have taken its full shape.

If you were to analyze what was inside the balloon, you would find your DNA. Your breath and DNA are inside of that balloon. It's the same way with God and His Word. God didn't just breathe on people and give them wonderful ideas to write about. God literally took human language on His lips like a balloon and breathed into it as He inspired the thinking of men and led them to write under the inspiration of the Holy Spirit. And like that balloon, the scriptures began to take form.

The first five books of the Old Testament, the minor prophets, the major prophets, the poetry books, and all the Old Testament began to grow. Then came the New Testament, and the balloon began to get bigger and bigger to include the epistles and the book of Revelation. Finally, when the Scripture was finished, God tied a knot at the end to seal everything inside. Here is what that means for you: The Bible isn't just a book that tells you about God — *God is actually in the Bible.* Just like your breath is inside that balloon, God Himself is in the Bible, contained within its words and pages. And when you open it up and begin to dive into the Scriptures, you begin to release the inspiration and power that is held within its pages.

The second part of the word "inspiration" in verse 16 — the Greek word *theopneustos* — is also important. It is the Greek word *pneustos*, and it comes from the root word *pneo*, which had three meanings when the apostle Paul used it in Second Timothy 3:16.

First, the word *pneo* was used to describe *creative energy* or *supernatural energy.* It is the same word used in the Old Testament Septuagint in Genesis 1:1 and 2 when the Spirit of God moved upon the face of the deep and released His divine power. Second, the word *pneo* was used in the Greek world during the First Century to describe *perfume.* This was a particular kind of perfume you would use to change the aroma of your house. Third, the word *pneo* was used in the First Century to describe *a flutist who put a flute to his lips.* Flutes are wonderful instruments, but if you don't breathe into them, they won't produce any sound. When a flutist begins to breathe into his instrument and move his fingers, suddenly that flute begins to produce the most marvelous, melodic music.

All of this is contained in the little word *pneo* — *creative power, fragrance,* and *music*. And this is what it means. **Number one:** When you open your Bible and begin to release the truths within it, it is filled with the creative power of God. If you need God to work a miracle in your life, your marriage, your children's lives, your home, or your finances, when you open up the Word of God and allow its power to flow into you, it releases divine, supernatural, and creative power.

Number two: If you have a stinking situation in some area of your life, you need Heaven's fragrance. When you open the Word of God and extract the truths within it, it releases the fragrance of Heaven into your life, and the smells of Heaven change the atmosphere of your home and your relationships.

Number three: If you don't like the sound or music you hear in your life, then dive into the Word of God because the Bible will fill your life with the sounds of Heaven. This is why you need to be committed to God's Word. We all need the creative power and fragrance and sounds of Heaven in our lives. If we will just dive into the Scriptures, the Lord's DNA will be released, and we will become partakers of all that God's powerful presence has to offer. *Amen!*

Let's take another look at Second Timothy 3:16, which says:

> **All scripture is given by inspiration of God, and is profitable for doctrine, for reproof, for correction, for instruction in righteousness.**

Notice the word "correction." It depicts *a person who has been knocked flat and who is lying on his back.* This person has been through a situation so difficult, or he has embraced some kind of thinking that is so wrong, it has knocked him flat. However, the use of this word "correction" in verse 16 tells us the Word of God has the power to pick up those who are lying on their backs and put them back on their feet again.

Again, we see the Bible isn't just the writings of men — *it contains the life, breath, and power of God!* And when you take the cap off the Word of God and release it, it takes people who have been knocked flat on their back

and supernaturally reestablishes them, putting them back on their feet
again.

Equipped to Last

Then we come to verse 17, which says:

**That the man of God may be perfect, thoroughly furnished
unto all good works.**

— 2 Timothy 3:17

The word "man" in this verse is the Greek word *anthropos*, and it refers to
any man, woman, or child who belongs to God. Verse 17 goes on to say, "That
the man of God may be *perfect….*" The word "perfect" is a form of the
Greek word *artios*, meaning *mature* or *complete.* And notice the final part
of this verse says "…*thoroughly furnished* unto all good works." The words
"thoroughly furnished" in Greek describe *a boat that is completely outfitted
for long-distance sailing.*

Imagine there is only one particular model of a boat. It's a simple boat
with no motor or sail. It may have oars, but it has no equipment, and
because it is ill-equipped, the boat can't go very far from the shore. Even
if it paddles out, it can't get to the other side and it could never survive
stormy weather. So every time this boat goes out a little, it has to keep
coming back. But you could take the very same model of boat and
thoroughly furnish it, and that is what the words "thoroughly furnished"
picture in verse 17.

You could give the boat a sail, a rudder, stronger oars, and all kinds of
equipment that suddenly transforms it into a vessel fit for long-distance
sailing. It would no longer be just a little boat that has to come back to
shore every time it paddles out. Instead, your boat would be so thoroughly
equipped that it could sail all the way to the other side. Not only that, if it
encountered any stormy weather on the way, it would be alright because
it has been equipped to deal with the fiercest of waves. This is a boat that
would make it all the way to the other side.

If you look at Second Timothy 3:1 and Second Timothy 3:17, you will
see that these verses are like bookends to this chapter. In verse 1, Paul
wrote, "This know also, that in the last days perilous times shall come."
This pictures your boat sailing to its last port with little time left for the
journey. And when you come to verse 17, Paul said, "That the man of God

may be perfect, thoroughly furnished unto all good works," telling you that if you have the Word of God working in your life, you will be okay because you are equipped like a ship that can sail through the roughest weather and the highest waves.

You are going to make it all the way to the end of the last days. You are not going to be shipwrecked along the way. Why? Because the Word of God has completed and thoroughly furnished you unto all good works. You are a believer who is *fully equipped* for the last days.

Two Kinds of Believers

Unfortunately, there are two kinds of believers in the Church today. First, there are the believers who get saved and never do anything. They are saved, but they are not really disciples. That is why, over and over again, these kinds of believers retreat in their spiritual life like a boat that tries to paddle away but has to keep coming back to the shore, and often they even become shipwrecked along the way.

But there is a second kind of believer who is a real disciple and student of the Word of God. This kind of believer is one who takes the Word of God into his life, allowing it to release its creative power and bring the fragrance and music of Heaven into his life. God's Word picks him up and puts him back on his feet again, equipping him in such a way that it doesn't matter what he faces at the end of the age. These believers are going to have everything they need to keep plowing through the waves and weather until they finally make it to the other side.

These are the two kinds of believers that are in the Church today: *those who are equipped* and *those who are not.* This is why you must stick to the Word of God. It has within it everything you need to transform your life and weather every storm. If you will open up the Scriptures and dive in, you will find that the Bible will release all these amazing things in your life — *and it will really change you!*

STUDY QUESTIONS

> Study to shew thyself approved unto God, a workman that
> needeth not to be ashamed, rightly dividing the word of truth.
> — 2 Timothy 2:15

1. What are the two kinds of believers in the Church, and what sets
   them apart?

2. In this lesson, you saw that the words "inspiration of God" in Second
   Timothy 3:16 are the Greek word *theopneustos*, a compound of the
   words *theos* and *pneustos*, which is a form of the root word *pneo*. What
   are the three meanings of *pneo* in verse 16, and why are these meanings significant?

3. What happens inside you as you spend time in the Word of God?

PRACTICAL APPLICATION

But be ye doers of the word, and not hearers only,
deceiving your own selves.
— James 1:22

1. How often do you really read your Bible? Do you treat it like the
   living breath of God or does reading your Bible feel like another task
   to check off your to-do list?

2. God has entrusted us with His Word. How can you make sure you are
   being responsible with what He has given you?

3. There are two kinds of believers: those who are equipped with the
   Word and those who are not. Take a moment to assess which kind of
   believer you are. What can you do to become an equipped believer?

LESSON 10

TOPIC

Come Boldly to the Throne of Grace

Editor's Note: This lesson was taken from Rick Renner's *Sparkling Gems
From the Greek, Volume 2*: July 29. *Sparkling Gems From the Greek* is a daily
devotional from the Greek language of the New Testament.

SCRIPTURES

1. **Hebrews 4:14** — Seeing then that we have a great high priest, that is passed into the heavens, Jesus the Son of God, let us hold fast our profession.

2. **Hebrews 4:15** — For we have not an high priest which cannot be touched with the feeling of our infirmities; but was in all points tempted like as we are, yet without sin.

3. **Hebrews 4:16** — Let us therefore come boldly unto the throne of grace, that we may obtain mercy, and find grace to help in time of need.

GREEK WORDS

1. "grace" — χάρις (*charis*): grace; historically, a favorable touch of the gods; an empowering touch that transforms

2. "obtain" — λαμβάνω (*lambano*): to seize or to lay hold of something in order to make it your very own, almost like a person who reaches out to grab, to capture, or to take possession of something; in some cases, it means to violently lay hold of something in order to seize and take it as one's very own; at other times it depicts one who graciously receives something that is freely and easily given

3. "mercy" — ἔλεος (*eleos*): compassion; a heart-wrenching emotion that compels one to action; deep-seated and unsettling emotions a person feels in response to something seen or heard

4. "find" — εὑρίσκω (*heurisko*): to find; usually points to a discovery made due to an investigation, scientific study, or scholarly research; a discovery made as a result of serious searching

5. "help" — βοήθεια (*boetheia*): a word with a military connotation; it can be translated to help meet someone's need, but first and foremost it was used to describe that moment when a soldier got into trouble; when his fellow soldiers were alerted to his dangerous situation, they were completely dedicated to the goal of going into battle to defend their co-fighter and fighting for his well-being, safety, and security; just hearing that a fellow soldier was in need was enough to beckon the other soldiers into battle and to motivate them to spare no effort in order to rescue him and bring him back to a place of safety and protection

SYNOPSIS

In this lesson, gain powerful insight into what it really means to "come boldly to the throne of grace," and realize that the help you need is only a touch of God's grace away.

The emphasis of this lesson:

The Bible says in Hebrews 4:14 that Jesus is your Great High Priest. He intercedes for you because He wants you to receive what you are believing for. Not only does the Bible say He is your High priest, but it also says Jesus understands and empathizes with you because He has stood in your place and has felt your fear, worries, and infirmities, and He wants you to be delivered from these things. That's why Hebrews 4:16 tells you to "come boldly unto the throne of grace." You *must* come boldly before Jesus and make your needs and wants known to Him in order to receive that touch of grace that only He can give to empower and transform your life.

Jesus is your Great High Priest — He wants to help you, but you must step out and take that help by faith. If you come boldly before the throne of grace and reach out to receive the help Jesus is offering, you will receive an infusion of mercy that will deliver you and enable you to do what you could never do on your own.

Jesus, Our Great High Priest

Hebrews 4:16 begins, "Let us therefore come boldly unto the throne of grace…," but what does that mean? To answer this question, we need to examine the verses surrounding verse 16. Let's begin with Hebrews 4:14, which says:

> **Seeing then that we have a *great high priest*, that is passed into the heavens, Jesus the Son of God, let us hold fast our profession.**

Jesus is our Great High Priest. We see a vivid illustration of this in Revelation 1 when John had a vision of Jesus, clothed in liturgical clothes, standing in the midst of seven golden candlesticks, which represented the seven churches of the New Testament. John saw Jesus standing there in the midst of the churches as the Great High Priest. Later in this chapter of Revelation, John described Jesus as having judgment on His face. Not only is He our Priest, but He is also our Judge. But Jesus is praying for us, and He wants us to respond so we never have to experience judgment. He is interceding for us because *He is our Great High Priest*!

Hebrews 4:14 concludes, "…Let us *hold fast* to our profession." To "hold fast" means *to wrap your arms around whatever it is you're believing for* — you hold on tight to it. This lets us know that Jesus is praying and interceding for you so that thing you're believing for will come to pass. The Bible goes on to say:

> **For we have not an high priest which cannot be touched with the feeling of our infirmities; but was in all points tempted like as we are, yet without sin.**
>
> **— Hebrews 4:15**

Jesus came to earth as a man. And in human flesh, Jesus faced everything you have ever faced and had every thought you've ever had. Any temptation you've stood against, Jesus had to stand against it too. Yet He was without sin. He had problems with His family and religious people; He had to resist the devil. In order for Jesus to be a merciful High Priest, He had to stand in our place; He had to understand the challenges we face, the emotions we feel, and the struggles that confront us —*Jesus confronted them all!*

Jesus Wants You To Be Bold and Direct

Jesus stood in our place, and because of that, He's touched by the feeling of our infirmities and wants us to come to Him to express our needs and desires. Hebrews 4:16 says:

> **Let us therefore come *boldly* unto the throne of grace….**

The word "boldly" is a form of the Greek word which describes *very frank, audacious direct speech*. This means when you come to the Lord, you don't have to beat around the bush — you are to be direct.

When Rick was a young man, he attended a wonderful church that really taught the Bible, but he wasn't taught about being authoritative and confident in prayer. That's why Rick grew up praying prayers like, "God, if it be thy will…." Rick felt like he was at the mercy of "if."

But in fact, if you know what the Bible says and understand that Jesus is on your side, when you come to Jesus in prayer you can be direct and audacious. That is what "come boldly unto the throne of grace" really means.

God isn't disturbed when you are straightforward with Him. In fact, God *likes it* when you are real and honest with Him. In the book of Genesis, when Lot was about to perish in the judgment that was coming down on Sodom and Gomorrah, the Bible says Abraham drew near to the Lord. Abraham knew he needed to draw near to the Lord because his nephew, Lot, was in trouble. Abraham prayed boldly to the Lord for Lot's life to be spared. And when he was finished communing with the Lord, He and Abraham went their separate ways (*see* Genesis 18:33).

The Bible never says God was offended by Abraham's straightforward manner of speech — in fact, He even called it *communion*. God likes it when we do business with Him! Considering this, when you read Hebrews 4:16, it is clear that when you come to the Lord, you are to be confident and to speak straightforwardly about what you feel, what you're facing, and what you need. You are not to be irreverent or disrespectful, but the Lord wants to hear exactly what you have to say. And you should always come to the Lord with Scripture because God responds to the Word of God.

The Transforming Power of the Lord's Touch of Grace

Let's revisit our key verse, which says, "...Come boldly unto the throne of *grace*...." The word "grace" is the Greek word *charis*. This word *charis* was borrowed from ancient Greek literature and existed before the writings of the New Testament. To understand the word "grace," you have to understand where this word first came from. The way the word "grace" — translated from the Greek word *charis* — was first used was very specific. It described *a person or group of people who received a supernatural touch from the gods of mythology.* In ancient days, they believed if the gods touched you, this touch would change you in such a way that it empowered you to be what you could never be by yourself and to do what you could never do by yourself.

In fact, the people who were touched by grace were so transformed that the people who witnessed the transformation would say, "Wow, that person is under a magic spell! He's under the touch of the gods!" That touch was *charis*, or the touch of grace.

Grace is an empowering presence, and when it touches you, it changes you to be what you could never be and do what you could never do before. You are so transformed that people could look at you and say, "You *must* be under grace, because that's not what you used to be like!"

Take Rick Renner for example. When Rick was a young man, he was easily intimidated and had a bad self-image. But when God's grace touched him, he changed. Rick is now confident and assured of who he is in Christ and boldly declares God's Word wherever he goes.

If you're dealing with any issues of fear, lack of confidence, or poor self-image, you need to come boldly to the throne of grace — *the throne is where His divine touch is conferred on those who seek it.* When God's grace touches you, it changes you. And suddenly, even if your situation doesn't change, *you* are changed in your situation! You are empowered to deal with your situation, to be different than you were before, and to do what you couldn't have possibly done without grace.

Grace is an empowering touch. When you come boldly to the throne of grace, you need to be ready for God to touch you, and you will become totally changed. *That is what grace is!*

But that's not the end of the verse! Hebrews 4:16 goes on to say:

> **…That we may *obtain* mercy, and find grace to help in time of need.**

The word "obtain" is a form of the Greek word *lambano*, which means *I take* and describes a person who reaches out by faith *to take something*. But it also means *I give*. God gives but you have to take it. In fact, God is giving you grace right now, but you have to reach out by faith and say, *I take it*!

If you need healing, God has given you healing, but you have to reach out to take it. If you need a financial blessing, God gives it, but you have to take it. If you need peace, God is imparting it, but *you have to reach out by faith and take it*. God is the giver, but you have to be the taker. And according to Hebrews 4:16, mercy is available to you, but you have to receive it.

Compassion With Action

Hebrews 4:16 says, "…That we may obtain *mercy*…." The word "mercy," the Greek word *eleos*, describes *a divine compassion that moves one to action*. God doesn't sit by and say, "Their situation is so pitiful. I just feel so sorry for them. I wish I could help them!" That's pity, not mercy. Mercy is a compassion that moves one to action. And God is compassionate when He sees your needs. He understands because Hebrews 4:15 tells us that Jesus has stood in our place. He's been touched with the feeling of our infirmity, so we can come boldly and tell Him what we're feeling.

Boldly declare the Scriptures, and tell the Lord, "Lord, You promised You would do this, and this is what I need You to do." He is moved to give you a touch of grace so you can obtain mercy — His compassion that moves on your behalf to change, rescue, and deliver you. That's really what the word "mercy" means; it is divine compassion that moves to action to make a difference in your life.

Verse 16 goes on to say, "...And *find* grace to help in time of need." The word "find" is a form of the Greek word *heurisko*, which describes *a very deep study* or *intensive scholarly research*. In other words, it means sometimes you have to really press in to get the help you need. You have to press in and say, "Lord, I'm not going to quit. I'm going to dig deep until I get it."

The word *heurisko* is also where we get the word "eureka." When you finally lay hold of the grace of God and the help He has to give you, you'll have a eureka moment, which means *I found it*! This moment will be euphoric as you're empowered by the grace of God and His mercy begins to rescue and deliver you from whatever it is you're facing.

But Hebrews 4:16 also says, "...And find grace to *help* in time of need." There's that empowering touch of grace again. But let's take a deeper look at the word "help." The word "help" is the Greek word *boetheia*, and it pictures *a soldier who's been struck down in war and is spotted by a fellow soldier who's in good shape, and rather than just walk off and leave the wounded, the able soldier comes to the wounded soldier's rescue.* The healthy soldier wraps his arms around the wounded soldier and says, "You're going to make it," and brings him back into a place of safety. Here we find a picture of Jesus' intercessory work as our Great High Priest referred to in Hebrews 4:14.

When Jesus sees we have fallen, He moves forward to intercede, or to act on our behalf. Jesus is the Great Warrior, and we're serving with Him. But in moments when we feel like we're down and out or there's been an attack against us and we don't know what to do, Jesus doesn't just stand by and pity us. He moves forward on our behalf as the Mighty Warrior He is and picks us up, wraps His arms around us, and releases divine grace to empower us. At that moment when we're in desperate need of a divine touch, Jesus releases His divine mercy and compassion and immediately goes to work to rescue us, deliver us, and set us free. *Jesus lifts us up in our time of need!*

On the program, Rick shared a moment in his life when Jesus empowered him in his time of need:

> Many years ago in Moscow, we had a great financial need in our ministry. We were preaching the Gospel on television like we still do, but at this particular moment, it seemed like we had a deficit of funds. It was time to pay the TV stations, and I didn't have the money to pay.
>
> I was brokenhearted that we were going to have to go off the air when people were hungry and waiting for the Word of God. The role of our partners is very significant, but at that time for some reason, a number of our partners had pulled back and our finances were down. I was going to have to go off the air, and I was devastated.
>
> Late one night after a meeting with the TV directors, I walked into Red Square — right in the heart of Moscow. I leaned against the railing and began to cry. It was so cold that it felt like my tears were going to freeze on my cheeks. But I cried and said, "God, you've got to help us. You sent me to this part of the world to bring the Word of God, and Lord, I don't want to disappoint these people. They're waiting for the Word of God. You've got to help us."
>
> I came boldly to the throne of grace, and I received grace. I received the divine touch at that very moment. It was like an infusion of power that came into me and changed the way I was thinking and changed my ability to be different from what I was feeling. Divine compassion and mercy were released to rescue us from this very tight space, and Jesus, my Great Warrior, stepped forward, wrapped His arms around me, and said, "Hey, I'm your comrade, and I'm going to deliver you in this time of need and make sure you have exactly what you need to get the job done." And I reached out by faith to take what Jesus was offering me.

Jesus is offering it all to you right now — mercy, grace, peace, healing, provision, and so much more. He's offering it to you, but it requires your response. You have to reach out by faith and take it, and if you do, you'll be empowered by grace and receive a divine infusion of mercy that will deliver you! Jesus will wrap His arms around you, put you back on your feet, and enable you to do what you cannot do and be who you cannot be on your own — all because of a divine touch of grace that you received by *coming boldly to the throne of grace.*

STUDY QUESTIONS

Study to shew thyself approved unto God, a workman that needeth not to be ashamed, rightly dividing the word of truth.
— 2 Timothy 2:15

1. What does Hebrews 4:14 mean by calling Jesus our Great High Priest?
2. What is grace, and what does a touch of grace from God do in our lives?
3. In this lesson, you saw that the word "mercy" is the Greek word *eleos*, which describes *a divine compassion that moves one to action.* Why is action so important? What is compassion without action?

PRACTICAL APPLICATION

But be ye doers of the word, and not hearers only,
deceiving your own selves.
— James 1:22

1. Have you ever been hesitant about boldly asking the Lord for what you need? Does knowing what "come boldly to the throne of grace" truly means make you more confident to be direct with Him?
2. Do you know anyone who is timid about asking the Lord for help? Drawing from what you read in this lesson, what would you say to that person to encourage them to be bold? Write down your answer and consider sharing what you learned with this person!
3. What did you think Hebrews 4:16 meant before reading this lesson? Has what you learned changed the way you will approach the throne of grace in the future?

CLAIM YOUR FREE RESOURCE!

As a way of introducing you further to the teaching ministry of Rick Renner, we would like to send you FREE of charge his teaching, "How To Receive a Miraculous Touch From God" on CD or USB format.

In His earthly ministry, Jesus commonly healed *all* who were sick of *all* their diseases. In this profound message, learn about the manifold dimensions of Christ's wisdom, goodness, power, and love toward all humanity who came to Him in faith with their needs.

☑ YES, I want to receive Rick Renner's monthly teaching letter!

Simply scan the QR code to claim this resource or go to: **renner.org/claim-your-free-offer**

🏠 renner.org

facebook.com/rickrenner • facebook.com/rennerdenise

youtube.com/rennerministries • youtube.com/deniserenner

instagram.com/rickrrenner • instagram.com/rennerministries_
instagram.com/rennerdenise